STYLE & VERNACULAR

A Guide to the Architecture of Lane County, Oregon

produced by the Southwestern Oregon Chapter,
American Institute of Architects

published by Western Imprints
The Press of the Oregon Historical Society
1983

Library of Congress
Cataloging in Publication Data

Main Entry under title:

Style & Vernacular
    Bibliography: p.
    Includes index
    1. Architecture — Oregon — Lane
County — Guide-books. 2. Vernacular ar-
chitecture—Oregon—Lane County—
Guide-books. 3. Lane County (Or.)—De-
scription and travel—Guide-books. I.
American Institute of Architects. South-
western Oregon Chapter. II. Title: Style and
vernacular.
NA730.072L368 1983   720′.9795′31
                              83-8019
ISBN 0-87595-085-x (pbk.)

Printed in the United States of America

Funds for this book were provided by the
Oregon Historical Society and by a grant
from the American Institute of Architects,
Washington D.C.

Typesetting: Editing & Design, Inc.
Printing: Ryder Printing

CREDITS

PROJECT DIRECTOR: Richard Glenn Williams AIA

PHOTOGRAPHY: Douglas Keep AIA, Paul Hansen
Gary Marshall, John Aldredge, Kevin Spady AIA, John Pratt

ARCHITECTURAL HISTORY: Philip Dole

WRITING: R.G. Williams, Philip Dole, Michael McCulloch

MAPS: Edward Waterbury AIA, William Seider AIA, Wayne Carley

BOOK DESIGN: Paul Hansen

DRAWINGS: Eric Gunderson AIA

COMPOSITION: Kevin Spady, Garry Fritz AIA, Douglas Keep

EDITING: Alice Hall
Bruce Hamilton, Oregon Historical Society

RESOURCE: Glenn Mason, Lane County Museum
Judith Rees, City of Eugene
Ellen Kotz, City of Springfield
Prof. Marion Ross, AIA
K. Keith Richard, U.O. Archives
Jerry Finrow, AIA,
   U.O. Dept. of Architecture
Gail Throop, U.S. Forest Service
A.D. McReynolds
Louis F. Pierce
Lee Everett
Mrs. Dove Trask, Cottage Grove
Mrs. Mary Johnston, Florence
Howard Buford

Special thanks for the help of Cheryl Steinmuller, Carole Irsfeld and Walt Biddle

CONTENTS

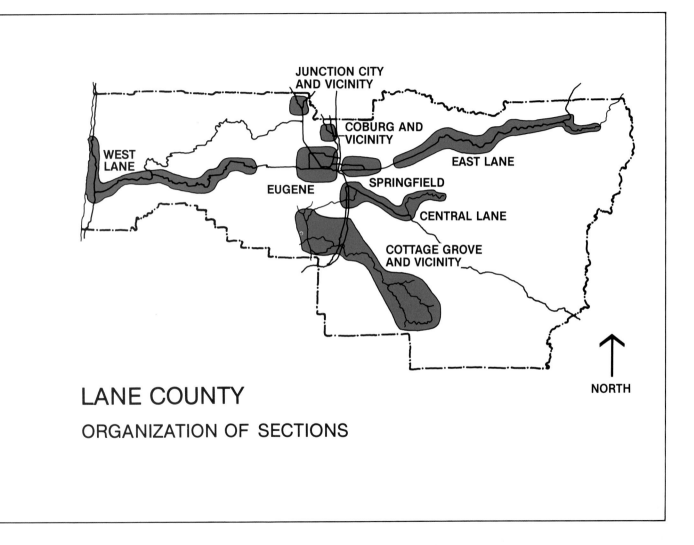

JUNCTION CITY
AND VICINITY

COBURG AND
VICINITY

WEST
LANE

EAST LANE

EUGENE

SPRINGFIELD

CENTRAL LANE

COTTAGE GROVE
AND VICINITY

NORTH

LANE COUNTY

ORGANIZATION OF SECTIONS

This book is dedicated to the memory
of Heinrich H. Waechter AIA

architect
artist
author
teacher
environmentalist

Born: October 2, 1907, Berlin, Germany
Died: April 17, 1981, Creswell, Oregon

INTRODUCTION

This *Guide* is a survey of the standing buildings and structures in Lane County. Selections were made by a jury of architects and historians with advice from interested people throughout the county. Selections were made for a variety of reasons and not always with unanimous agreement. Some examples typify the different types of buildings and structures to be found in the county. Most were chosen as representative of architectural design values of their time—their existence adds continuity to our historical perspective. Others were included simply for their design or, occasionally, to make a point.

Not all buildings of historical importance could be included and preference was given to those reasonably intact and without destructive changes. Limitations of space have caused many significant houses and commercial buildings to be omitted and representative examples shown in their place. Selections made in this *Guide* are not intended to suggest the full extent of historically significant buildings or to limit preservation efforts.

The introductory passages trace a number of factors that have influenced the face of our surroundings. Though references are occasionally made to architectural styles and features, detailed descriptions of stylistic terms are beyond the scope of the *Guide*. Several publications made expressly for this purpose are cited in the "Suggested Reading" section. Readers are advised, however, that clear, "textbook" examples of the early styles are not often found in buildings outside of the larger cities—especially those built before 1900 by builders who were not thoroughly familiar with their characteristics or origins and who tended to lend more conventional or vernacular expressions to their work. Where style features were copied from earlier buildings or publications, they were often modified or combined to suit the owner's fancy or the builder's needs.

Several buildings and structures have been listed on the National Register of Historic Places because of their special historical value. The designation (NRHP) identifies these.

The *Guide* is intended to give the visitor a comprehensive visual image of the architecture of Lane County, but its first purpose is to expand the residents' perceptions of their familiar daily environs —whether by armchair study or by tours to the listed sites.

Those who choose to visit the sites are reminded that the listing of a building in the Guide *does not imply that it is open to the public. Please respect the rights of those who occupy the property.*

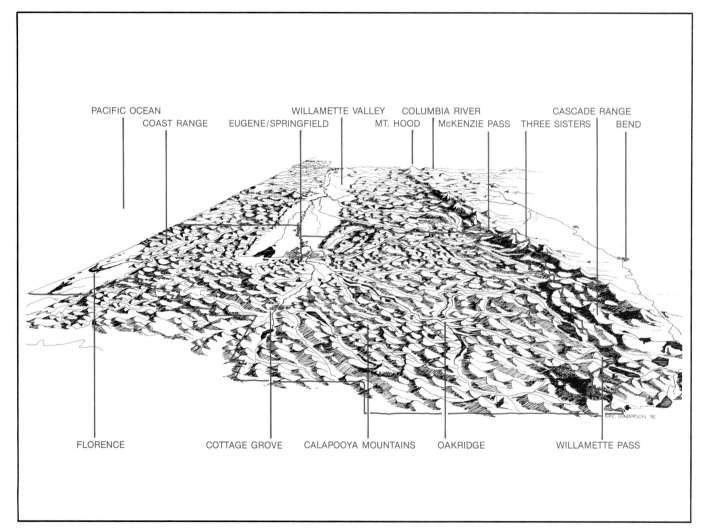

PACIFIC OCEAN

COAST RANGE

EUGENE/SPRINGFIELD

WILLAMETTE VALLEY

MT. HOOD

COLUMBIA RIVER

McKENZIE PASS

THREE SISTERS

CASCADE RANGE

BEND

FLORENCE

COTTAGE GROVE

CALAPOOYA MOUNTAINS

OAKRIDGE

WILLAMETTE PASS

ERIC GUNDERSON '82

LANE COUNTY

SETTLEMENT AND GROWTH

In 1851 when it was first defined as a part of the newly created Oregon Territory, Lane County extended as far· east as the Rocky Mountains. Its boundaries were reduced considerably by the time Oregon became a state eight years later, but they still contain a diversity of landforms, climates and vegetation matched by few other counties in the United States.

Beginning at the Pacific coast, with its mixture of broad beaches and rocky headlands, the county extends eastward some 120 miles, over the eroded Coast Range that shelters the relatively populous Willamette Valley, continuing up again through the thick, forested west slopes of the Cascade Range to 10,000 foot-high volcanic peaks standing among glaciers and fields of lava.

These landforms affected settlement patterns within the county. The mountains channeled early travel from the north and south over separate routes along the coast and through the Willamette Valley where settlers came in search of farmland. Movement from east to west was very difficult until much later when roads and railroads allowed settlement to spread out from the valley into the lower mountains on both sides. Coastal communities grew independently along coastal trails, while scattered communities in the higher Cascades came with the development of roads across the passes.

THE WILLAMETTE VALLEY

Sometime after 1811, during their first incursions into the Willamette Valley, trappers and fur traders of the Hudson's Bay Company found small bands of the Calapooya and Siuslaw Indian subtribes living in semi-permanent villages along the Willamette River and its tributaries. The Valley was then a land of tall grass, and the trappers were probably the first outsiders to witness Indians practicing field burning to capture game and expose a favored forage of wild seeds. By the time the first white settlers began to arrive, the Indian population had been reduced by disease. Most of those surviving were moved to reservations in the 1850s. Except for that being found in scattered archeological sites, there is little remaining evidence of the Indian presence in Lane County.

Encouraged by promises of fertile land free for the taking, settlers had begun to move to the West in the late 1830s. A man who arrived before the end of 1850 was allowed 320 acres of land (640 if he was married) under the Donation Land Claim Act. In 1851 the grants were reduced to 160 and 320 acres. These grants ceased in 1855. The act provided for more land than was needed for farming, and many saw the prospect for profit in sale and development. Because the act also set aside land for schools, it helped form the base for a mature and stable population centered around the family—a base far different from that of mining camps and other transient population centers elsewhere in the West.

Until the Central Military Road was cut through the Cascades in 1852 (near present State Highway 58), settlers usually came to the southern Willamette Valley from the north along the east and west-side territorial roads, after first coming west to Oregon City. They chose elevated land back from the river to avoid flooding —a problem that was to plague valley development for years.

Small towns sprang up quickly. Wherever a road crossed a river, someone established a ferry. The ferry points drew settlers, a school, a church, a general store and often a post office. Without so much as a building permit or an environmental impact statement, settlements were born.

Eugene began in this way. So did Lancaster. Each wanted to be the county seat. One succeeded and the other now contains a solitary gas station. Other settlements were even less fortunate than

Lancaster. Places such as Trent and Cloverdale remain in name only.

The business of early Lane County was agriculture. Rivers and streams irrigated fields and powered flour mills. At that time the timber that stood all around was little more than an obstruction to farmland. Without adequate means of transportation, timber products would not become the county's major industry until the 1900s.

Shipping on the Willamette River never developed significantly in Lane County, though the river was navigable as far south as Eugene. From the 1850s, daily overland stage lines boasted six-day trips between Sacramento and Portland, but the dirt roads were only seasonally passable. Reliable transportation had to await the railroads, first from Portland in 1871, then to California with connections to the

East in 1883. Then immigration spiraled, and agriculture and logging boomed with access to distant markets.

BEYOND THE VALLEY

Beginning in the late 1870s, homesteading began to draw people out of the valley into the foothills of the Coast and Cascade ranges. Extension of the railroad into these areas freed the lumber industry from its dependence on rivers, allowing access to new timberlands. As a result, many logging camps became towns around 1900. Among these were Marcola, Mabel, Westfir, Mapleton and Saginaw. Much later, the Great Depression drew more people out of the valley to find jobs in the logging and home industries.

The mountains were another matter. On the west side of the Coast Range,

Florence grew independently along the coast trail and prospered from fishing and lumber shipping in the last two decades of the nineteenth century. Vacationers from the valley first began to visit the coast in those decades, well before the railroad crossed the mountains in 1914. The coast highway with its succession of concrete bridges was built in the 1930s.

Routes east out of the valley into the Cascades faced a greater barrier. Only pioneer routes and the McKenzie Pass trail, built to move livestock to eastern rangeland, challenged the Cascades until 1866, when recreational needs pushed roads up the McKenzie River to hot springs and fishing holes. Other roads were constructed following the discovery of gold north of Blue River and in the Bohemia mining district southeast of Cottage Grove during the latter half of the century. But it was not until 1926 that the railroad was extended beyond Oakridge, over the Willamette Pass summit, finally completing an east-west route across the county.

BUILDING IN LANE COUNTY

The pattern of settlement seen in Lane County was not unique in the Pacific Northwest. Settlement varied with conditions. The same is true for Lane County's architecture. Styles and building types found here are generally typical of the region—although there are individual places that are special or rare. Of greater importance is the fact that representative examples of architecture from nearly every period can still be seen in Lane County. (A number of buildings are included in this *Guide* primarily because they are rare survivors of certain periods.)

Of those examples of early architecture which are missing today, the most notable are the two types of temporary houses usually built by each settler (the first of three homes commonly built in their first 10 or 20 years in Lane County). Soon after his arrival, a settler put up a simple pole shelter or log cabin to weather the first winter or two. Next, a larger house of hewn logs sufficed until a more permanent house of sawn lumber was constructed in the 1850s or '60s. Functionally more complete than the first two structures, the sawn lumber houses usually followed designs remembered from the settlers' earlier homes in the East. Of the hundreds which once stood on claims throughout Lane County, only about 15 remain.

After 1870, builders and owners based their designs on the many style or pattern books which had become popular. But, because owners and builders adapted, modified and combined features and styles seen in these books, their influence was anything but conforming. Modifications included subtle changes in orientation and detail better suited to the local climate and materials than the eastern models, as well as those prompted by simplification or personal fancy. In consequence, the expressions that resulted were often more vernacular than stylistically faithful. Some are quite plain, representing common forms typical of their time. Others are highly individual. Each is important for the way in which it continues our historical perspective.

Lane County's rural churches also express this range in the interpretation of pattern-book sources. Commonly built in the Gothic Revival Style at the end of the nineteenth century, they are remarkable for their variety in detail.

The succession of building styles that formed much of the basis for architectural design for almost a century is well documented in buildings which have survived throughout the county. Several are among the best in the region. The Spores house near Coburg and the 1853 County Clerk's office in Eugene—a rare, surviving early government building—remain as fine examples of the Classical Revival Style. Many houses followed the popular Gothic Revival Style, perhaps best seen

in the Peters-Liston-Wintermeier house—one of the finest examples of this style in Oregon. A few houses adopted the Italian Villa Style though the Italianate Style was more common to early commercial facades such the Kyle building in Florence. Many buildings of this period benefited from the work of craftsmen such as Rev. Charles Hamilton Wallace, a circuit riding preacher and an extraordinary mason. Deady and Villard halls, two important early buildings on the University of Oregon campus now listed as National Historic Landmarks, illustrate different approaches to the Second Empire Style. They were the first significant projects by architects, then from Portland, in the county.

As the twentieth century approached, the usually ornate Queen Anne Style be-

came popular, often for its air of prestige as in the Shelton-McMurphey house. Many fine examples of each of these periods remain in the residential architecture of Cottage Grove and Junction City, but Eugene lost dozens to a second generation of building in the proliferous Bungalow Style, common until 1920-30. The Soults-Westfall house, one of the best examples, is also rare for its L-shaped duplex form.

Around 1900, Lane County gained its first architect of note in John Hunzicker, whose work in varied Revivalist styles is best expressed in Springfield's Douglas house. Still, it remained for Ellis F. Lawrence to bring the historically based styles to full flower. A Portland architect and dean of the School of Architecture and Allied Arts at the university from

1916 to 1946, Lawrence left many lessons in the application of style on the campus and beyond. His power plant in Leaburg in an Art-Deco motif and Hope Abbey Mausoleum in Eugene, a rare example of the Egyptian Revival Style, illustrate the broad range of his work. Lawrence's colleague at the school, W.R.B. Willcox, left a legacy of a different kind—a generation of architectural students charged with pursuing an architecture responsive to its own time and place. These students became the architects who shaped much of Oregon's modern architecture in the 1940s, '50s and '60s. Of all modern work in the county however, the best known is that of Portland architect and A.I.A. Gold Medal recipient Pietro Belluschi. His churches in Cottage Grove and Eugene are well known professionally throughout the world.

The county-wide scope of this *Guide* lets us look, too, at a number of specialized structures that underwrote the development of the county and its resources. The evolution of barns and farm buildings

is interesting for its mixture of imported technology, native genius and esthetic achievement. Lane County's major industry saw another kind of evolution in its best example of "architecture-as-machine"—the sawmills. Forest Service structures built under Depression era work programs at recreational and administrative sites in the national forests bear, in their Rustic Style construction, a special character and sensitivity toward their surroundings that is rarely achieved now.

Among all structures, none were more essential to the development of the railroad and to the life of the early settlements than bridges. No early examples remain but traditional forms have continued, particularly for covered wooden bridges. While not unique as a class, Lane County's covered bridges are unique in their number. At 20, more exist here than in any comparable geographic area in the country. And along the coast, the reinforced concrete bridges that were so vital to the highway that finally linked the isolated coastal communities, are a part of a statewide system of bridges built between 1919 and 1938 that won international recognition for their designer, bridge engineer Conde B. McCullough. Many employed innovative structural concepts but they are more widely appreciated for their graceful forms and integral Art Deco design elements. Considered together, they present a rare and highly successful synthesis of engineering and architecture that is among the best of its time.

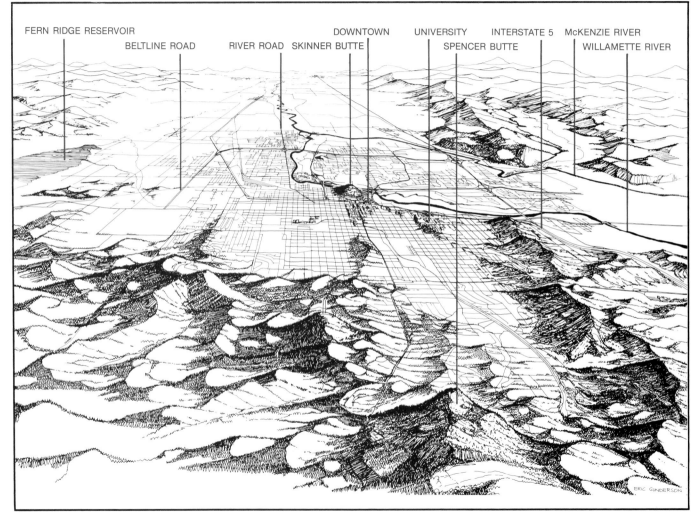

FERN RIDGE RESERVOIR
BELTLINE ROAD
RIVER ROAD
SKINNER BUTTE
DOWNTOWN
UNIVERSITY
SPENCER BUTTE
INTERSTATE 5
McKENZIE RIVER
WILLAMETTE RIVER

ERIC GUNDERSON

EUGENE

A study in contrasts, Eugene's mosaic of buildings gives visual testimony to the city's growth and change. The downtown area includes such diverse elements as the 1982 Performing Arts Center, a nearby 1914 railroad station (now a restaurant), the 1884 Smeede Hotel and a large 1977 parking structure.

A vast number of early commercial buildings have been destroyed but, in contrast to many cities, Eugene still contains a few buildings from its earliest period in the 1850s and '60s. Many that have been spared from the wrecking cranes of change are making new contributions to the economic life of the city through adaptation and restoration.

Because so many of the early buildings were destroyed, altered or moved from their original sites, it is difficult to trace the city's development from styles and locations seen today. However, decisions made by the first residents did establish the general pattern of today's city. The city grid is still based on the axis of Willamette Street, aligned on the first plat between Skinner Butte to the north and Spencer Butte to the south. The plat was known as "Skinner's Mudhole" when Eugene's first plan for land development reminded settlers of the importance of building away from the flood-prone Willamette River. Since then, new nodes of growth have occurred, in hopscotch fashion, on scattered spots of high ground around the city.

In 1846 Eugene Skinner put up his cabin, the first building in the settlement, on the west shoulder of Skinner Butte, but city growth did not begin there. Skinner and Charnelton Mulligan donated parts of their adjoining land claims to establish the county seat in 1853. Four blocks were set aside for county use and became the nucleus of the present government center adjacent to the park blocks. Another forty acres, "thrown in" as land the county could sell, became the commercial district. These areas grew and changed, but they have retained their original function.

Another area important to Eugene's development grew and then declined. The Millrace, built by Hilyard Shaw in 1851 to provide water power for flour and sawmills, flourished as an industrial site until electricity replaced water power as an energy source.

The founding of the short-lived Columbia College in 1856 and the University of Oregon in 1876 formed two new nodes of growth on dry knolls well away from town. Beginning in the 1870s, newcomers, now arriving by train, built

homes west of downtown and on the east side of Skinner Butte—the first purely residential areas.

All this development occurred around the early roads that served the city. Coburg Road (linking ferries near the present Ferry Street Bridge and at Armitage) and River Road were the main routes to the north. They were connected by Blair Boulevard running diagonally to 8th Street, which intersected Willamette Street. Eleventh Street later grew as a

link between the westside residential area and the university. (Numbered "streets" were later changed to "avenues.")

Other transportation systems contributed significantly to Eugene's growth, and each succeeding system influenced the pattern of development. Eugene's position at the head of Willamette River navigation played an important part in the city's initial growth. Farmers brought their produce to Eugene for shipment to markets downriver until 1871, when the railroad reached Eugene, offering cheaper, more dependable shipment of goods.

To accommodate visitors and new residents, hotels, a railway station, and businesses sprang up downtown north of

6th Avenue. Industrial development along the tracks spread to the west. When trucking superseded railway transport, businesses abandoned the downtown buildings near the tracks and scattered outward along Franklin Boulevard and the early roads. Between 1891 and 1927, a streetcar system within Eugene (and to Springfield after 1910) influenced growth south of downtown and in the university area. In the latest generation of change, freeways and their interchanges have attracted commercial development like Valley River Center to the fringes of the city.

Just as new buildings replaced old and as patterns of development changed

within the city, so the natural environment changed with growth and development. Eugene was once part of an almost treeless, grass-covered valley. The giant shade trees that are now such an integral part of the city's character were planted by early residents.

Eugene citizens have become increasingly concerned about uncontrolled growth and have taken an active role in planning for the city's future. In 1967, a citizens' group developed a set of community goals to guide development. Adopted by the city as the 1990 Plan, the main objective is to prevent urban sprawl by containing city services within an urban service boundary. More recently, an initiative measure stopped the continued development of freeways that had begun to bisect neighborhoods.

Another of the community's goals concerned protection of the city's natural ridgelines. Eugene is contained on the south by a crescent of hills and on the north by Skinner Butte. This series of ridges and hilltops forms a distinct visual edge, providing a sense of orientation from any point within the space it nearly surrounds. For many years, the Willamette River also defined the northern edge of city growth. but urban development has gone beyond this natural barrier and now reaches toward others. Nevertheless, Eugene's unique setting will continue to give the city a sense of place and community scale.

To the pedestrian, the city core today forms a tangible link with the past through a lively mixture of buildings from many periods. This character—like the visual connection between Willamette Street and the buttes—should be selectively preserved and enhanced as a historical benchmark that remains constant amid continual change.

Because the dynamics of change within Eugene have obscured its historic pattern of development, this part of the *Guide* is divided into nine sections and presented in the way the city is seen today.

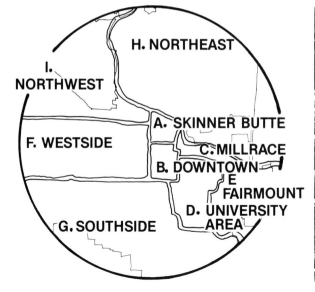

A. SKINNER BUTTE

Eugene began here in 1846 with the construction of Eugene Skinner's cabin. Its exact location and appearance are unknown but plaques placed on the west side of the butte near 2nd and Lincoln mark the vicinity of the site.

The old residential area identified now as the East Skinner Butte Historic Landmark Area appears today to have been the place of earliest growth. In fact it was not, although several houses built elsewhere before 1875 and relocated here around 1900 contribute to this impression. In spite of its nearness to Millrace industry, development here did not begin in earnest until the 1880s —well after many other parts of town were established. Still, it is the earliest neighborhood that remains relatively intact. Recent construction, some sensitive to its surroundings, has brought about a sharp contrast of old and new.

From 1888 to 1905 a University of Oregon observatory overlooked this area from a site on the east crown of the butte. Along the river, the land that is now a park was once occupied by a small sawmill and a shipyard.

After 1900, the area south of the butte became the gateway to the city as travelers' accommodations and warehousing developed around the railroad. The area's importance declined along with that of rail travel, and as traffic increased on 6th and 7th avenues it was all but disconnected from downtown.

Recent restoration and adaptation, especially in the "Fifth Street District," has brought many of the old buildings back to life and begun to reestablish the commerical link with downtown. If a physical link ever restores the historical connection of downtown with the butte, it will be through the two-block site of the Performing Arts and Convention Center complex astride Willamette Street between 6th and 7th avenues.

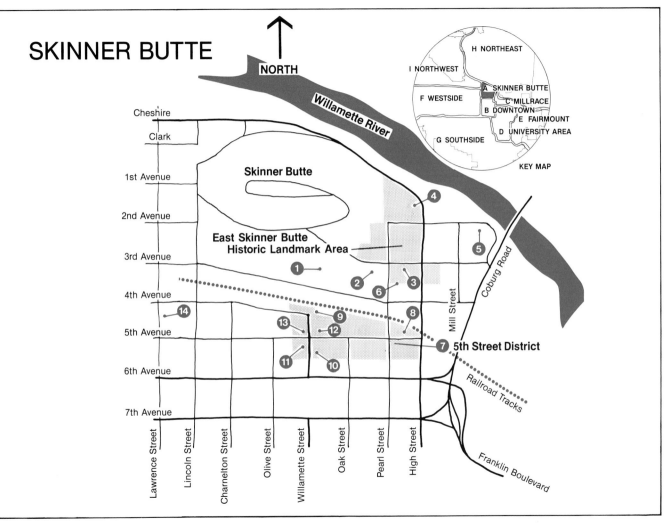

SKINNER BUTTE

NORTH

Willamette River

KEY MAP

H NORTHEAST
I NORTHWEST
A SKINNER BUTTE
C MILLRACE
F WESTSIDE
B DOWNTOWN
E FAIRMOUNT
G SOUTHSIDE
D UNIVERSITY AREA

Skinner Butte

East Skinner Butte
Historic Landmark Area

5th Street District

Cheshire
Clark
1st Avenue
2nd Avenue
3rd Avenue
4th Avenue
5th Avenue
6th Avenue
7th Avenue

Lawrence Street
Lincoln Street
Charnelton Street
Olive Street
Willamette Street
Oak Street
Pearl Street
High Street
Mill Street
Coburg Road
Railroad Tracks
Franklin Boulevard

1 **SHELTON-McMURPHEY HOUSE** **1880**
303 Willamette Street
W.D. Pugh, architect
Lord Nelson Roney, builder
Mature trees now soften the commanding situation
of Dr. T.W. Shelton's house, once known as the
"Castle on the Hill." Its elaborately detailed woodwork and hexagonal tower are features common to
the Queen Ann Style of architecture.

Oregon Historical Society

LORD NELSON (NELS) RONEY
1853-1944

Few builders of any period have had
as much impact on Lane County construction as Nels Roney. From 1886 to
1905 he built nearly every important
building in Eugene. Many are gone now
but they encompassed all types—commercial, educational, religious, public
and residential. Those that survive include Villard Hall, for which Roney was
construction superintendent, the Shelton-
McMurphey house (pictured left), the
Tiffany Building at 8th and Willamette and
the Roney Building at 5th and Willamette.
Still remembered are the First National
Bank, now extensively remodeled as the
45 West Building at Broadway and Willamette, and the 1898 County Courthouse, which dominated the downtown
until it was replaced by the new courthouse in 1959.

These buildings might have provided
career enough for most, but Roney is
much better known as the most prolific
builder of covered bridges in Oregon's
history. From the time he submitted his
first bid following the flood in 1881 until
about 1925, Roney built nearly 100
bridges in Oregon. Many, of his own
conservative design, served well over an
average lifespan of 35 years. With con-
sistently low bids, he virtually dominated
the field in Lane County for forty years.
Roney's last bridge was taken down in
1953, but some of the foundations of the
1910 streetcar bridge between Eugene
and Springfield can still be seen.

2 YA-PO-AH TERRACE 1968
350 Pearl Street
Graybrook & Bradbury, architects
W.H. Shields Construction Co., builder

This high-rise building helped to bring the issues of design review and height restriction into sharper focus in Eugene. Used for housing elderly people, the building drew criticism for its conspicuous presence, which was alleged to diminish the presence of Skinner Butte and to intrude on a historic neighborhood. It is an example of lift-slab construction — a technique whereby all concrete floor slabs are cast in a stack on the ground and raised into position on their supporting columns.

3 COGSWELL-MILLER HOUSE 1884
246 E. 3rd Avenue

This example of the Rural Gothic Style of architecture was relocated from a site near the present YA-PO-AH Terrace. It is intact except for the porch added in 1910. Miller was prominent in the development of Florence, Oregon, and platted the Fairmount area of Eugene.

5 **OFFICE BUILDING** 1972-74
460 E. 2nd Avenue
Moreland/Unruh/Smith, architects
R.A. Chambers Construction Co., builder
Sculpture by Ray Edwards
Sited to take advantage of both north light and views of the Willamette River, part of this building was designed for the architect's own offices. Balconies, skylights and outdoor terraces are carved from the simple shed forms, giving it a pleasant scale.

4 **HIGH STREET ROWHOUSES** 1980
140 High Street
Unthank Seder Poticha Architects
Frank Blain, Jr., builder
At a density of 25 units per acre, this project for 18 connected rowhouses was central to Eugene's attempt to limit urban sprawl by encouraging development in the central city. Its location in the East Butte Historic Landmark Area brought opposition from neighborhood and preservation groups. The project demonstrates the variety of views and living spaces possible on a compact site.

6 **J.O. WATTS HOUSE** c.1893
335 Pearl Street
Still quite intact, the corner tower and bay windows of this unusual house are characteristic of the Queen Anne Style while its form and two-story porch are more closely related to Italianate structures.

7 FIFTH STREET DISTRICT 1900s
E. 5th Avenue from High to Willamette streets

Recently revitalized as a commercial area, the Fifth Street District was originally a group of warehouses built against the railroad after 1900 to serve early industry. As industry moved elsewhere, the district declined until 1971 when the first shops and offices opened in remodeled spaces. More came and now the area, with its "new functions in old buildings" ambiguity, offers a lively alternative to the downtown core and suburban shopping malls.

It is still popularly known by its original name although "avenues" replaced numbered "streets" years ago.

8 THE GRANARY BUILDING c.1905
259 E. 5th Avenue
1971 Remodel: Unthank Seder Poticha Architects
Frank Blain Jr., builder

Led by its architect-owners, the remodeling of the Granary Building gave impetus to the redevelopment of the Fifth Street District. Now converted into offices and a restaurant, the original grain bins have been made into unusual seating areas for the restaurant.

10 EAGLES BUILDING 1906
521 Willamette Street

An unusual commercial front with its design based on the Mission Style. Note the imitation rafter poles projecting from the upper facade.

11 U.S POST OFFICE 1938
520 Willamette Street
Gilbert Underwood, architect

Some Art-Deco Style features, particularly the blue terra-cotta on the east front, are evident in this government building from the New Deal era.

9 SOUTHERN PACIFIC RAILROAD DEPOT 1908
Willamette Street at 4th Avenue

The third passenger depot to be built at this location appears to have been a design prototype for Southern Pacific stations of this period. These often followed the designs of H.H. Richardson's 1880 stations in the east, though far more simply detailed. The site includes an express office, bunkhouse and remnants of its landscaped south entrance.

12 OREGON ELECTRIC DEPOT 1914
27 E. 5th Avenue (NRHP)
Doyle, Patterson & Beech, architects
Moore Bros., builders
Now adapted for use as a restaurant, this depot was built for an interurban electric railway that served Eugene between 1912 and 1933. Borrowing heavily from the Classical and Georgian Revival styles, the building is notable for its carved stone detailing and prominent entrance of arched windows.

13 LANE HOTEL 1903
now the LANE BUILDING
488 Willamette St. (NRHP)
Van Dorn McFarland, builder
Although built near the railway station one year before the first automobile appeared in Eugene, this building served as a hotel until 1978. Opened as the Gross Hotel, and later, Griggs and Palace, it was known as the Lane Hotel for 50 years. A continuous railing once edge the veranda roof of this Commercial Italianate design typical of its time.

14 PLINY SNODGRASS HOUSE 1880s
437 Lawrence Street
Elaborate detailing and varied siding treatments characterize this Queen Anne Style residence.

streets where it grew for 50 years as a mixture of businesses and dwelling spaces, some above or adjoining the family store. After 1900, growing commercial needs forced residents out of the area and many of the early houses were relocated from their original downtown sites. Piecemeal change continued until the construction in 1969 of Valley River Center raised an economic challenge to the old commercial center. This threat triggered a wholesale effort to preserve the downtown core. Entire blocks were leveled and rebuilt while the spaces between were remade into a pedestrian shopping mall. Parking garages were also built from a plan that is still incomplete.

In their broad-brush approach, however, the plans for both government and commercial centers would have swept away many buildings of historical importance. Fortunately, a few were spared and today their place among newer buildings has found more support.

B. DOWNTOWN

Two adjoining building groups form the nucleus of downtown. The government and commercial centers were both created by the donation of land for a county seat in 1853. Neither has moved its location appreciably and both are as visually significant as they ever were.

The present government center resulted from a proposal, volunteered by a group of local architects in 1954, to bring all government buildings together into a single core. New and larger facilities were needed. Successive county courthouses had occupied the original site at 8th and Oak streets while other government offices existed in scattered locations. Although land was never set aside for this purpose, the idea was realized when city, state and federal offices eventually adjoined the new County Courthouse—the first building constructed (1959) under the plan.

The original commercial center lined Willamette Street from 5th to 11th

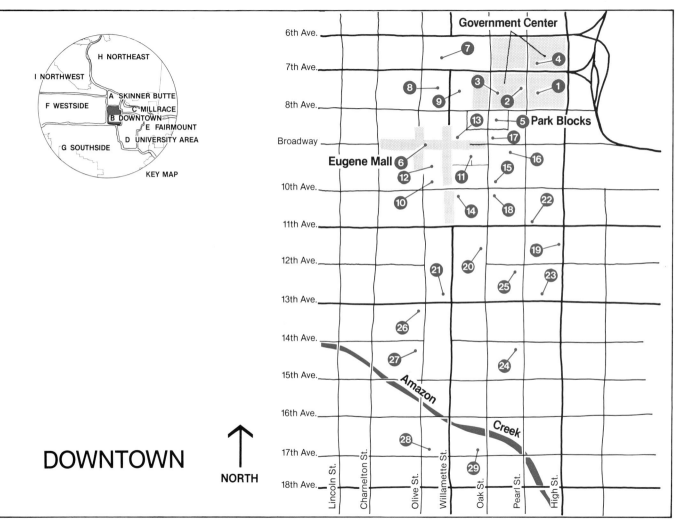

DOWNTOWN

NORTH

Government Center

Park Blocks

Eugene Mall

KEY MAP

H NORTHEAST

I NORTHWEST

F WESTSIDE

A SKINNER BUTTE
C MILLRACE
B DOWNTOWN
E FAIRMOUNT
D UNIVERSITY AREA

G SOUTHSIDE

6th Ave.
7th Ave.
8th Ave.
Broadway
10th Ave.
11th Ave.
12th Ave.
13th Ave.
14th Ave.
15th Ave.
16th Ave.
17th Ave.
18th Ave.

Lincoln St.
Charnelton St.
Olive St.
Willamette St.
Oak St.
Pearl St.
High St.

Amazon Creek

1 **EUGENE CITY HALL** 1964
777 Pearl Street
Stafford, Morin & Longwood, architects
Gale M. Roberts Co., builder
Sculpture by Jan Zach
The result of a design competition, the building
houses most city offices as well as the police and
fire departments on a plaza above a parking level.
The council chambers, seating 160, symbolically
occupies the center of the plaza while the various
offices surround the edge along a covered walk.

2 **PUBLIC SERVICE BUILDING** 1977
E. 8th Avenue and Pearl Street
Unthank Seder Poticha Architects
Simpson Construction Management
Sculpture by Dimitri Hadzi
This building is notable for its modest scale and
design for energy conservation. Deciduous vines at
the perimeter are intended to provide summer shad-
ing and flat-roof collecting ponds circulate water to
storage tanks to balance heating and cooling needs.
The roof is a landscaped terrace with a pedestrian
bridge connection to City Hall. The building contains
works by numerous local artists.

3 **LANE COUNTY COURTHOUSE** 1959
125 E. 8th Avenue
Wilmsen & Endicott, architects
Gale M. Roberts Co., builder
Built on the same site as its predecessors, the
courthouse was significant as the first major new
building in the eventual development of the Government District—a modern renewal that spread to the
Commercial District as well. Though modern in exe-
cution, the building retains much of the formal symmetry traditional in earlier American courthouses.
Its brick interior is of special interest.

4 FEDERAL OFFICE BUILDING & COURTHOUSE 1975

211 E. 7th Avenue
WEGROUP Architects
Todd Building Co., builders
Sculpture by Robert Maki

This building makes a wall-like edge in forming the northeast corner of a complex of government buildings. While the building itself is formal, it is at the same time invitingly accessible to the public. Its precast concrete exterior by Morse Bros. is of exceptional quality.

5 PARK BLOCKS (1959) & PARKING STRUCTURE (1960)

E. 8th Avenue & Oak Street
Wilmsen & Endicott, architects
Lloyd Bond, landscape architect
J.M. Steinmuller, Jr., builder (Park Blocks)
Gale M. Roberts Co., builder (Parking Structure)
Sculpture by Tom Hardy and Jan Zach

The park blocks form an open link between the complex of government buildings to the north and east and the commercial area to the south and west. Historically a focal point of the downtown area, they were redeveloped on the site of an earlier park in conjunction with the present courthouse. The two-level county parking structure is an unobtrusive companion to both.

Once an uneasy mixture of people, cars and trucks, the Mall has made a total commitment to the pedestrian as a part of a renewal plan to maintain the economic vitality of the downtown core. While the open space of the streets was traded for a few too many objects and amenities in the relatively narrow space, the fountain structure has proved to be a versatile centerpiece for a variety of musical and dramatic events. Time and change have allowed many of the building fronts to adapt to the more personal character of the Mall and strengthen its edge, though all still draw a firm line against the open space. Some of the better new storefronts include Seymour's, Danish Imports and Norm Thompson's.

6 **EUGENE MALL** 1971
Broadway & Willamette Street
Mitchell, McArthur, Gardner & O'Kane, landscape architects
Geo. Rockrise; Morin & Longwood, consulting architects
Gale M. Roberts Co., builder

8 PARCADE PARKING STRUCTURE 1977
W. 8th Avenue & Willamette Street
Lutes Sanetel Architects
Minden Const. Co., builder

The bold use of color and graphics, the glassed-in exterior elevators and strong geometric composition balanced around expressive stairways clearly proclaim the importance of the user over the automobile in this finely crafted building. Sloped surfaces within the building are minimized for alternate use if the need for parking is solved by other means in the future.

7 EUGENE CENTRE 1982
Willamette Street, 6th to 7th avenues

HULT CENTER FOR THE PERFORMING ARTS
Hardy, Holzman & Pfeiffer, architects
Jaffe Acoustics, Inc., acousticians
R.A. Chambers Const. Co., prime contractor
Todd Building Co., construction managers

EUGENE HILTON HOTEL
Gaber-Jacoby, architects
Vik Const. Co., builder

EUGENE CONFERENCE CENTER
WEGROUP Architects
Noell Associates, interior designers
Todd Building Co., builders

Although the various buildings in the Centre were designed as separate projects, common criteria were established to give unity to the overall development. Concerns for exterior materials were subordinated to interior development to make best use of available funds. The Hult Center contains two performance halls of vastly different character reflecting different purposes. The intimate 515-seat Soreng Theater is an angular counterpoint to the Baroque allusions of the spacious 2537-seat Silva Concert Hall whose design was intended to recall the curvilinear forms of earlier European halls. Acoustic performance in each is rated excellent. The hotel and conference center were designed to be mutually supportive, both functionally and visually. The conference center and Hult Center each contain artwork commissioned by competition.

9 **SMEEDE HOTEL** 1884-5
767 Willamette Street (NRHP)
George H. Park, builder
1973 Remodel: Unthank Seder Poticha Architects
Frank Blain, Jr. builder
Once associated with the ultimate in Eugene's early social and cultural life, the Smeede (originally Baker's Hotel) was saved from demolition and adapted for use by shops and offices in 1973. A stucco finish was applied to the original brick Italianate Style facade in 1892 and the vaulted metal canopy was added to the front in the early 1900s.

10 **THE ATRIUM** 1973
99 W. 10th Avenue
Moreland/Unruh/Smith, architects
Churchill Development Corp., owner/builder
This building type—commercial and office spaces ringing a skylit atrium—became a popular commercial building form in the 1970s. It turns its back to the outside to focus on its own internal ''street'' complete with trees, protected ''sky,'' walkways, cafes, balconies, etc., little of which is perceptible from the city outside. Originally intended primarily as commercial centers, such mini-shopping centers have tended to draw private office functions to their upper floors.

11 **DANIELSON, DRISCOLL & HESS,**
ARCHITECTS OFFICES 1978
1 E. Broadway Mall Walk
Danielson Architects
John Pratt, builder
This is an infill structure built to occupy a ''leftover'' space between adjoining stores. Its only facade is its 14-foot main entry doorway. Light enters the building from above through skylights and monitors (vertical windows in vertical building projections).

12 LUCKEYS CLUB CIGAR STORE 1974
933 Olive Street
Ken Morin & Assoc., architects
Hiatt Const. Co., builder
Signs by Goettling Sign Co.
A fine interpretation, in modern terms, of one of Eugene's oldest saloons—displaced by Urban Renewal from its original 1911 location on Willamette Street. Many of the interior fixtures were moved intact.

13 EQUITABLE SAVINGS BUILDING 1962
899 Willamette Street
Lewis Crutcher, architect
George A. Moore & Assoc. and
J.M. Steinmuller, Jr. Co., builders
This building forms the northeast edge of the central fountain space of the downtown mall. The steel structure, unusual for the region, is open to the south and west. Metal screens provide sun protection and soften the building's edge.

14 SCHAEFERS BUILDING 1929
1001 Willamette Street (NRHP)
Hunzicker & Smith, architects
Truman Phillips, designer
Stein Brothers, builders
Like many downtown buildings whose ground floor fronts have been heavily altered, this building retains fine detail on its upper story that often escapes notice. In this case, the facades of multi-colored brickwork laid with chevron motifs running vertically combine with horizontal cast concrete features to achieve a decorative scheme that emphasizes the structural bay system of the building. Some of the lower level detail, including a stepped concrete arch, remains at the northeast corner.

15 CITIZENS BUILDING 1975
975 Oak Street
Callison, Erikson & Hobble, architects
Charles Pankow, Inc., builder

This building serves two urban functions—as a lively foil for the somber Telephone Building to the south and as the centerpiece in the only downtown-feeling stretch of street in Eugene—Oak Street from 8th to 11th. The repetitive pattern of arched window bays in precast concrete gives the building a timeless quality that will blend well as downtown buildings grow up around it. The ground floor banking space, designed by the San Francisco office of Skidmore, Owings and Merrill, architects, is especially worth seeing.

16 QUACKENBUSH BUILDING 1902
160 E. Broadway (NRHP)

Until recently, Quackenbush's Hardware Store operated continuously on this site. The store is one of very few early commercial buildings remaining downtown. Its appearance and layout are virtually unchanged from the time of establishment and features the original wire cashier-cage system—a tradition well known in this area.

18 PACIFIC N.W. BELL TELEPHONE CO. 1928
112 E. 10th Avenue
1975 Remodel: WEGROUP Architects
Eldon Shields Const. Co., builder

Although it mainly houses telecommunications equipment, this building has the size and location of a traditional office building. The latest of several remodelings incorporates commercial activity at street level behind shallow arcading. The pleasant proportions, warm brick color and masonry detailing both soften and humanize the structure.

17 SOUTH PARK BUILDING 1975
101 E. Broadway
Herbert and Keller, architects
Vik Const. Co., builder

One of the few truly urban buildings in town, the structure is inviting from almost any angle. The diagonal pedestrian way through the building connects the park to the north with the busy intersection of Oak and Broadway, enhancing both places. Projecting bays, pitched roofs, casement windows and wood finishes were all employed to achieve a personal scale. In addition, the building was designed to be demountable to allow maximum recycling of materials in the future.

19 OFFICE BUILDING 1974
1158 High Street
Unthank Seder Poticha Architects
Frank Blain, Jr., builder

Located in a neighborhood undergoing transition from residential to commercial uses, this building provides pleasant pedestrian access from street to alleyway. With its steeply pitched shed roofs, it is a good example of the use of simple, inexpensive building materials.

21 KENNELL-ELLIS STUDIO BUILDING 1947
1280 Willamette Street
Robert Wilmsen, architect
Waldo S. Hardie, builder
In this excellent example of the Art Moderne Style, the smooth flowing lines of the curved soffit, the un-interrupted balcony and handrails and the faceted windows all intensify the speed and continuity of the street. This style was characteristic of buildings which looked to industrially produced items such as airplanes and ships for their streamlined imagery.

20 FIRST CHRISTIAN CHURCH 1911
1166 Oak Street
George W. Kramer, architect
Welch Bros., builders
In this design by a New York architect, the portico in the Ionic order and the pediments which occur on each side are all clear expressions from the Classical Revival period. The dome is central to its large sanctuary which originally held up to 2500 for evangelical services. The bell tower was added in 1926, matching the dome in detail. The two locust trees in front were planted in the 1860s.

22 BENJAMIN FRANKLIN SAVINGS AND LOAN 1973
201 E. 11th Avenue
Stanton, Boles, McGuire and Church, architects
Vik Const. Co., builder
This is one of many buildings seen today whose designs are derived from their corporate identity—in this case, one whose tradition is foreign to its time and place.

23 APARTMENT BUILDING 1930s
259 E. 13th Avenue

This building is an example of early higher density housing in Eugene. It makes use of materials and forms characteristic of apartment buildings of the time. These include an arched entry, brick of different colors and steel casement windows.

24 SOULTS-WESTFALL DUPLEX 1916
1412 Pearl Street

This unique, L-shaped duplex was built for the related Soults and Westfall families. Essentially a highly articulated Bungalow, its massive, horizontal forms and multiple gables with pronounced eaves of intersecting and projecting boards are imitative of the Western Stick Style of architecture popular in California in the early 1900s.

25 **DANIEL CHRISTIAN HOUSE   c. 1855**
170 E. 12th Avenue
Daniel Christian III, probable builder
Cottage-sized farm houses such as this were a common type of Oregon pioneer home. Though moved from its original site across the street to the north, the house still stands on its original donation land claim and is designated a City Historic Landmark. The porch, siding and front openings are later additions, but the building shape and roof are original with Classical Revival eave details of handmade lumber.

26 **EUGENE PUBLIC LIBRARY   1958**
100 W. 13th Avenue
Hamlin & Martin, architects
Gale M. Roberts Co., builder
A fine composition of elements, boldly opposing horizontal and vertical masses in careful balance. Its modest scale and large windows against the street invite public use.

27 **FIRST METHODIST CHURCH   1967**
Olive Street & W. 14th Avenue
Morin & Longwood, architects
Vik Const. Co., builder
Artwork by Harold Balazs
The design makes a conscious effort to recall the scale and illumination of large, early churches, and to interpret these in modern forms and materials. The roof is pierced with onyx glass set in pre-cast concrete panels executed by Chas. E. Nelson of Willamette Greystone from designs by Harold Balazs. The carved doors, altar hanging and cruciform relief on the east facade are also by Balazs.

28 17TH & OLIVE TOWNHOUSES 1980
W. 17th Avenue & Olive Street
Threshold/A group of architects
Cedar Sand/Elizabethan Enterprises, builders

Originally an existing apartment house and two separate single family houses, this project has been integrated through infill into a single complex. It achieves high density in a low density neighborhood through the use of thoughtful planting and the repetition of carefully scaled building elements.

29 U.S. NATIONAL BANK 1961
17th & Oak Branch
Wilmsen, Endicott & Unthank, architects
Gale M. Roberts Co., builder

The proliferation of branch banks after 1950 gave rise to a new genre of bank buildings as they moved away from their traditional downtown settings and into residential and low-density surroundings. Personal scale, an informal nature and warm, tactile materials are all characteristics of this fine example.

C. THE MILLRACE

The Millrace has long been a focal point of Eugene both in pride and controversy. To provide waterpower for industry in the early 1850s Hilyard Shaw cut a channel between two old riverbed scars on his land claim. A number of mills attached themselves to the lower end of the race (where the south end of the Ferry Street Bridge now stands). Logs and farm products, floated in from the river via the Millrace, helped establish Eugene businesses. Houses were built along 11th and Garden avenues after 1900 by residents who found the Millrace an agreeable backyard amenity.

Occasional floods and disputes with property owners put the future of the Millrace in doubt. A flood brought the last mill wheel to a stop in 1928, and the mills converted to electricity. By this time, however, the Millrace had become a popular site for university recreation and social events. Fraternities and sororities located on its banks. But troubles continued to plague the race. Recreation dwindled during World War II, another flood left it dry, and construction at the Ferry Street Bridge and elsewhere reduced its flow to a trickle. Threats were made in the 1950s to fill it in.

Nevertheless, the upper Millrace has survived to face a future as unclear as its water. Its salvation may rest in the Emerald Canal—a proposed link to join the Millrace and the Amazon Slough near 15th and Charnelton through 10 blocks of the city. If constructed, this canal would complete a system extending to Fern Ridge Reservoir west of the city. It would stabilize water flow and provide flood control, while adding a landscape feature of exciting potential to the center of the city.

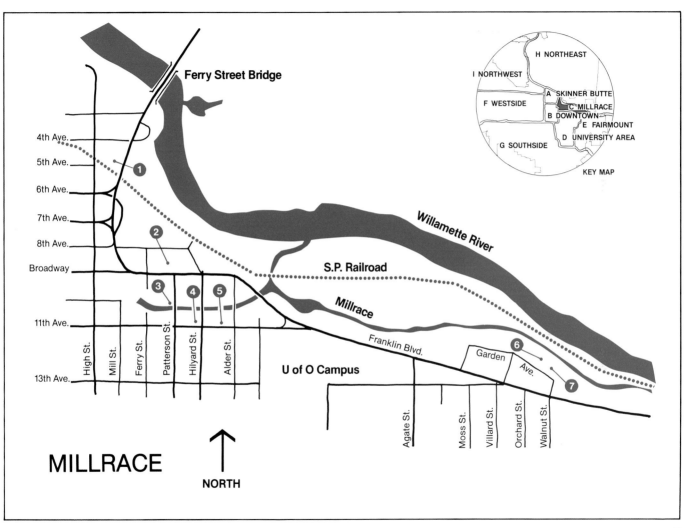

MILLRACE

NORTH

Ferry Street Bridge

Willamette River

S.P. Railroad

Millrace

Franklin Blvd.

U of O Campus

4th Ave.
5th Ave.
6th Ave.
7th Ave.
8th Ave.
Broadway
11th Ave.
13th Ave.

High St.
Mill St.
Ferry St.
Patterson St.
Hilyard St.
Alder St.

Agate St.
Moss St.
Villard St.
Orchard St.
Walnut St.

Garden Ave.

KEY MAP

H NORTHEAST
I NORTHWEST
F WESTSIDE
A SKINNER BUTTE
C MILLRACE
B DOWNTOWN
E FAIRMOUNT
D UNIVERSITY AREA
G SOUTHSIDE

1 EUGENE MILL & ELEVATOR CO.   c. 1895
east of E. 5th Avenue and High Street

Only this grain elevator remains of all the industrial buildings that once derived their power from the Millrace. The company's site, which included a flour mill, warehouses and another elevator at one time, stood at the northwest corner of the industrial complex. The Millrace split into three tail races which threaded the complex just east of here and rejoined before flowing out to the river.

2 ABRAM'S CIDER & VINEGAR MILL   c. 1880
602 E. 8th Avenue

Though it did not use the Millrace for power, Abram's Mill was once a part of the industrial complex that formed in this area for that purpose. In its prime, the mill dried 150 bushels of plums and made over 50 barrels of cider per day.

3 UNIVERSITY INN   1968
1000 Patterson Street
Pratt, Henderson and Box, architects

This building is a good example of thoughtful siting, careful massing and poured-in-place concrete construction. Its lawns respect the edge of the Millrace while its mass forms a wall between noisy Franklin Boulevard to the north and the quiet Millrace area to the south.

4 **ALPHA PHI HOUSE   1923**
1050 Hilyard Street
Lawrence and Holford, architects
Masterfully executed in the Tudor Revival Style, this large sorority house offers further evidence of Ellis Lawrence's sure sense in the use of appropriate style for residential architecture.

6 **WILLIAMS HOUSE   1931-32**
1989 Garden Avenue
Eyler Brown, architect
Like its neighbors to either side, this English Cottage Style house is typical of the residential character developed along Garden Avenue between the two world wars. Large back yards sloped down to join the Millrace. Brown designed a number of Eugene houses while he was a Professor of Architecture at the University.

5 **DR. A.W. PATTERSON HOUSE   1903**
now the PHI KAPPA PHI HOUSE
751 E. 11th Avenue
In style, size and date, this house reflects the fashionable residential character of East 11th Avenue. Its Moorish gable arch frames a ''Venetian'' window. Dr. Patterson's varied career included the original platting of Eugene and thirty-four years of pioneer medical practice. The house was the setting for the 1979 film, ''Animal House.''

7 **HOWARD HALL HOUSE   c. 1930**
1991 Garden Avenue
Howard Hall, architect
A low stucco house of the English Cottage Style —emphasized by sharply pitched assymetrical roofs and bands of small-paned wood casement windows.

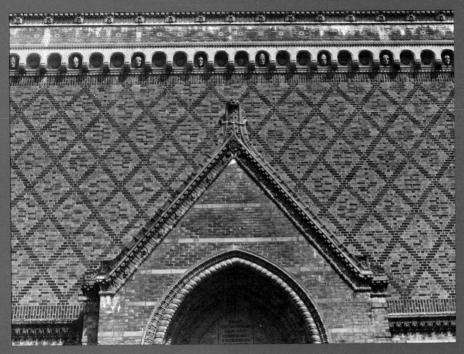

D. UNIVERSITY AREA

In 1876 the University of Oregon began as a single building on a nearly treeless rise, well removed from the east edge of Eugene. Deady Hall stood alone until Villard Hall joined it ten years later. Growth was confined to this area until 1890, when the purchase of the Collier house and farm across 13th Avenue opened the way to expansion toward the south.

The campus was still north of University Street in 1922 when University President Prince Lucien Campbell and Dean Ellis Lawrence combined their visions to design a classical form campus masterplan. The plan was abandoned soon after with Campbell's passing, but Lawrence continued to design many buildings along visual axes that still exist. The most important axis extends from the Library to the Dads Gates and traffic circle at the northwest corner of campus. This was once seen as the formal entrance to the university, with a railway station planned just outside on the tracks that then ran along Franklin Boulevard. Minor axes also remain west of Deady Hall to the center of 12th Avenue, north and south of Johnson Hall and along the east-west walks ending at the ''fishbowl'' in the student union.

Inevitably, the campus stimulated development beyond its edges. The first growth occurred along 11th Avenue, joining the university with the town, and especially with the residential area west of downtown (an area where faculty lived and commuted for thirty years until its own residential districts began to form east to Fairmount Boulevard and south along University Street).

This area also includes two early cemeteries. The Pioneer Cemetery at 18th and University, established by the Odd Fellows in 1873, contains graves of many early residents, as does the Masonic Cemetery, established in 1858 at University Street and 25th Avenue.

In 1978, both Deady and Villard halls were named as National Historical Landmarks in addition to their listing in the National Register of Historic Places.

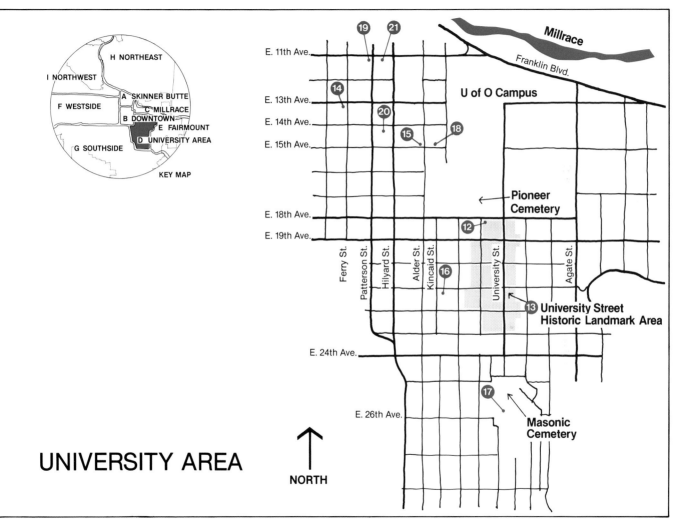

UNIVERSITY AREA

NORTH

1 **LAW CENTER** 1970
E. 11th Avenue & Kincaid Street
Wilmsen, Endicott & Unthank, architects
Todd Building Co., builder
Adjoining the Dads Gates, the building anchors the
northwest corner of the University campus. Its expressive exterior identifies each major element—
the library to the north with its projecting study
carrels, the lecture halls enclosed by large blank
masses on the west and the shuttered faculty offices above.

2 **DEADY HALL** 1873-76
University of Oregon Campus (NRHP)
William W. Piper, architect
W.H. Abrams, builder
Begun in 1873, but not completed for three years
because of a lack of funds, Deady Hall was the first
building for what was then called the Union University Association. The building was named for Judge
Matthew P. Deady, the first president of the University's Board of Regents, and housed the entire University for ten years. Piper was among the first
architects in Oregon to use the then popular Second
Empire Style. Usually very ornate, Deady is an excellent example of how the style could be achieved
with minimal resources. While its exterior is virtually
intact, the interior has been completely rebuilt.

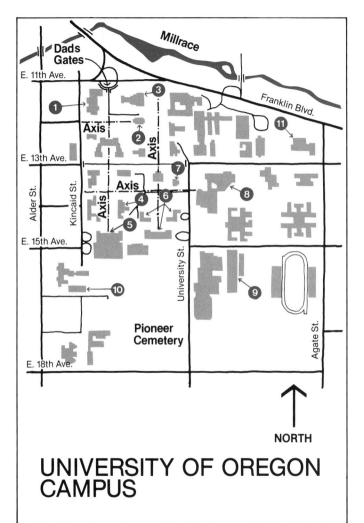

Millrace

Dads Gates

E. 11th Ave.

Franklin Blvd.

①

③

Axis

②

Axis

⑪

E. 13th Ave.

Axis

⑦

Alder St.

Kincaid St.

Axis

④

⑥

⑧

⑤

University St.

E. 15th Ave.

⑩

⑨

Agate St.

Pioneer Cemetery

E. 18th Ave.

NORTH

UNIVERSITY OF OREGON CAMPUS

3 **VILLARD HALL   1886**
University of Oregon Campus (NRHP)
Warren H. Williams, architect
W.H. Abrams, builder
Lord Nelson Roney, const. supt.

Following the precedent set in Deady Hall, Williams designed this building in the Second Empire Style—sometimes called the General Grant Baroque. With more funds, and perhaps a more thorough knowledge of the French precedent, Villard Hall comes closer to the ideal than does Deady Hall. It is now the most sophisticated example of this style remaining in the state. The exterior is almost intact except for the theater added to the west side in 1949. The interior was totally rebuilt at the same time. Its name honors Henry Villard, the first benefactor of the University.

U.O. Archives

ELLIS F. LAWRENCE F.A.I.A.
1879-1946

The period of the 1920s and 1930s was one of significant growth for the University of Oregon and its surroundings. Many large, important buildings were erected in a variety of revivalist styles popular then throughout the country. Since most of these buildings remain, the image of that period is still very evident today.

The great majority of these buildings was the work of one man, Ellis Lawrence. Lawrence lived in Portland, where he was a principal in the architectural firm of Lawrence and Holford. In 1914, University President Prince Lucien Campbell asked him to establish the School of Architecture. He became dean of the school two years later, while still continuing his practice in Portland (for 30 years he commuted two days a week by train to his campus office). This unusual arrangement also made him the architect for all University of Oregon buildings between 1916 and 1939; these eventually included Education (1917), Condon Hall (1923), McArthur Court (1926), Straub Hall (1928), Esslinger Hall (1936), Chapman Hall (1939) and all buildings at the U.O. Medical School in Portland, in addition to others listed this *Guide*.

His work manifested itself beyond the campus and included several fraternity and sorority houses, the now-demolished Heilig Theater and the Power Plant at Leaburg. Lawrence also designed many buildings throughout Portland and at Whitman College in Walla Walla, Washington.

Lawrence had an unfailing insight into the appropriate use of historical styles. His Mausoleum with an Egyptian motif, Art-Deco reliefs for a power plant and living quarters in Colonial and Tudor Revival styles offer special evidence of his ability to apply a broad vocabulary of design to a diverse set of building needs.

He also believed in the integration of the arts and crafts in architecture—a purpose best demonstrated in Lawrence's University Library and Art Museum shown opposite. Supported by President Campbell, this belief was an important influence in the organization of the new School of Architecture and Allied Arts, as the departments of architecture, fine arts and crafts were brought together to unite the visual arts and encourage collaborative work.

4 MUSEUM OF ART   1928-33
University of Oregon Campus
Lawrence & Holford, architects
Ross B. Hammond, builder

Since the Museum of Art forms a part of a quadrangle begun with Condon Hall in 1924 in a modified
Lombardic Romanesque Style, it was natural to follow that style in the general lines of the building.
Many details, however, suggest Islamic architecture
and the late Gothic period in northern Italy. The del-
icately ornamented main facade contrasts sharply
with the bare brick masses on the sides and rear.
Left plain in the expectation of future additions,
these facades anticipate modern forms. The Museum was built from private contributions to house the
Murray Warner Collection of Oriental Art.

5 UNIVERSITY LIBRARY   1937
University of Oregon Campus
Lawrence & Holdford, architects
Ross B. Hammond, builder

The Library joins the Museum of Art and Prince
Lucien Campbell Hall in the south quadrangle to
terminate the main campus axis, begun with the
Dads Gates to the north. Its design continues the
suggestion of the late Italian Romanesque seen in
the Museum, but with more modification in detail,
some becoming almost modernistic. The entrances
and interior are enriched with bronze gates, mural
paintings and sculpture funded by the Works Prog-
ress Administration in 1937.

6 **HENDRICKS HALL (1918), GERLINGER HALL (1921), SUSAN CAMPBELL HALL (1921) COMPLEX**
University of Oregon Campus
Lawrence and Holford, architects
Rushlight & Hastrof, builders (Gerlinger)

This complex forms one of the first groups designed by Lawrence and Holford after they established the first plans for the University in 1914. The architects chose the Georgian Colonial Style for these buildings, perhaps thinking that a domestic character was more appropriate to women's dormitories and a gymnasium than the heavier Lombardic Romanesque they were using elsewhere. All three buildings are considerably altered on the interior, although Gerlinger still has its monumental stair and handsome lounge on the second floor.

7 COLLIER HOUSE 1886
now the FACULTY CLUB
E. 13th Avenue & University Street

This Italianate Style residence was built for University professor George Collier on farmland that stood outside the campus of that time. It was purchased by the University in 1890 and became the home of three university presidents before becoming the Faculty Club in 1940. An addition was made to the west in 1963.

8 ERB MEMORIAL STUDENT UNION
1950, 1974
E. 13th Avenue and University Street
1950 building: Lawrence, Tucker & Wallman, architects
1974 Addn: Colburn & Sheldon, Lutes & Amundsen, architects
Todd Building Co., builder

This building is essentially a composite of two contrasting structures. The quiet elegance of the original building is a good foil to the exuberant addition with its skylighted, promenade ramp and lively detailing. The area on the west, known as "the fishbowl," becomes a porch looking out on to campus activity. The diagonal path under the building forms a gateway linking the active central campus with the interior residence lawns to the south and east.

10 **COLLEGE OF EDUCATION ADDN.** 1980
University of Oregon Campus
Martin, Soderstrom & Matteson, architects
John T. Moody & Sons Const. Co., builder
This building represents the first complete new project on campus to use the "Pattern Language" approach to design developed by Christopher Alexander in his book *The Timeless Way of Building* (see Suggested Reading). The building continues the scale, materials and allusions to style seen in the existing Education buildings and includes a commons and scholars' walk—once traditional in academic buildings.

9 **TENNIS AND HANDBALL COURTS** 1971
E. 15th Avenue east of University Street
Unthank Seder Poticha, architects
Howard Nelson Const. Co., builder
South-facing roof sections screen these courts from direct sun and rain, allowing students to take advantage of the mild Eugene climate to play "outdoors" year round. The design for this entirely prefabricated structure underwent wind-tunnel testing to predict its reactions to wind and rain.

12 **CENTRAL LUTHERAN CHURCH** **1959**
E. 18th Avenue and Potter Street

Pietro Belluschi, architect
Vik Const. Co., builder

Designed by Belluschi (an internationally known Oregon architect), this is one of a series of Lutheran churches made from similar materials and derived from the same design principles. The main sanctuary sits firmly on the corner with the education wing to the south. Belluschi also designed churches in Cottage Grove, Salem and Portland at about the same time.

11 **OREGON HALL** **1975**
E. 13th Avenue & Agate Street

Zimmer, Gunsel, Frasca Partnership, architects
Juhr & Sons Const. Co., builder

This building is sited to assist in forming an eastern gateway to the University of Oregon campus. A south-facing terrace is framed by the student services wing to the north and an administrative tower to the east. Its colorful interior is especially effective when seen at night from 13th Avenue.

13 UNIVERSITY STREET HISTORIC LANDMARK AREA

Like most of the university campus, this area was once a part of the Fielding McMurray land claim. Realizing its potential for growth on the edge of the university, the Lane County Investment Company acquired the land in 1907 for development.

Lots sold briskly from 1907 to 1929 as an intra-urban migration brought many residents away from the Westside residential area to the growing University district. A new electric street railway connected the area with downtown between 1907 and 1927. Growth escalated in 1924 along with that of the city and the university.

Sales were heavily promoted while building quality was regulated by deed restrictions, enforced setbacks and minimum costs. European beech trees were planted along the streets to achieve a ''Parisian character.''

The majority of the houses were designed in the revival styles popular in the 1920s—Colonial, Tudor and Mission—with few of the Bungalows popular in the Westside. The oldest house, built in the 1900s at 1992 Potter, is in the Queen Anne Style. Several fraternity and sorority houses done in the Tudor Revival Style stand unobtrusively among the large houses. With little building occurring between 1929 and 1940, the few modern houses that exist in the area create a more distinct departure from the older styles.

U.O. Archives

WALTER ROSS BAUMES WILLCOX A.I.A.   1869-1947

During 25 years in Eugene, W.R.B. Willcox designed only four buildings that were built. But his influence on his students, and their many buildings throughout the Northwest and beyond, is inestimable.

Like Dean Ellis F. Lawrence, who brought him here in 1922 to head the Department of Architecture, Willcox was an architect with many projects to his credit from his practices in Vermont and Seattle. But, unlike Lawrence, he was, first, a teacher—one with unusual impact on his students and the educational process of that time.

For many years, architecture schools across the country were entrenched in the Beaux-Arts tradition—a French academic system that promoted historical building styles, usually within monumental and classical settings, while emphasizing technique over theory and group competition over individual growth. Willcox contributed to the break with that system, arguing for reason over rules and judgement over authority. He believed, as did Louis Sullivan, that architecture was an expression of the values, aspirations and character of the society that produced it and that it should reflect the mind and thought of its own time. Under his guidance, Oregon became

a model for other schools, as it left traditional methods and developed new concepts in architectural design and education more appropriate to a new time and place.

To his students, however, the man was as important as his theories. Willcox had a unique regard for each student as an individual and left an indelible mark on all who studied under him.

The few buildings that Willcox designed offer an interesting contrast to those created by E.F. Lawrence during the same period. Lawrence found appropriate expressions for his architecture in the more literal use of traditional styles. While Willcox's buildings make poetic allusions to traditional forms (as did the early work of Frank Lloyd Wright and Bernard Maybeck), they belong to no specific style, instead reflecting his commitment to an architecture that might be universally understood. However, both Willcox and Lawrence shared a commitment to the integration of the arts and crafts in their buildings.

Of his four Eugene buildings, the three that remain are shown in this *Guide*. One of his best, the Westgate building (or College Side Inn) at 13th and Kincaid, was replaced by the U.O. Bookstore in 1964-65.

14 **FIRST CONGREGATIONAL CHURCH** 1925
Now THE WILLCOX BUILDING (NRHP)
492 E. 13th Avenue
W.R.B. Willcox, architect
Earl M. Drew, builder
A wealth of traditional characteristics, from the building masses, fenestration and cloister-like porch to the carved and turned exterior wood trim have their roots in the Mediterranean and California Mission styles. The innovative use of gunite—a blown-on cement finish—can be traced to Willcox's acquaintance with Bernard Maybeck. Students, university faculty and parishioners all contributed to the arts and crafts detail found in the hand-painted lighting fixtures and stenciled trusses over the sanctuary.

15 **KAPPA ALPHA THETA HOUSE** 1924
now the PHI GAMMA DELTA HOUSE
791 E. 15th Avenue
W.R.B. Willcox, architect
Wm. T. McDermott, builder
The exterior walls which step back at each level on the south facade add subtle articulation to the building mass and form deep window recesses in lower floor spaces. The vertical shaft on the east end originally contained a fire pole for quick exiting.

16 JAMES SCOTT McMURRAY HOUSE c. 1885
930 E. 21st Avenue

Built on a 200-acre farm, this house was moved two blocks north around 1915. Its basic form is Gothic Revival, but originally it had Queen Anne gable detail. The bricks for this house as well as for Deady and Villard halls were manufactured near the Pioneer Cemetery—then a part of the 600-acre farm of McMurray's father which most of the University now occupies.

17 HOPE ABBEY MAUSOLEUM 1913
E. 26th Avenue at University Street (NRHP)
Lawrence and Holford, architects
Portland Mausoleum Co., builder

Built of concrete with a stucco finish, the Mausoleum is described as the only truly monumental example of the Egyptian Revival Style in Oregon. The adjoining Masonic Cemetery, established in 1858, contains the plots of many prominent early residents including Eugene Skinner, Gov. John Whitaker and Nels Roney.

18 SIGMA KAPPA HOUSE 1950
851 E. 15th Avenue
Wilmsen and Endicott, architects
Waldo S. Hardie & Sons, builders

The carefully composed exterior of this sorority house is a clear expression of the International Style —a significant departure from the traditional styles common to fraternities and sororities until that time.

20 WEST UNIVERSITY NEIGHBORHOOD PARK 1979
E. 14th Ave. between Hilyard and Patterson
Diethelm and Bressler, architects &
landscape architects
Soter Landscape Contractors & volunteers, builders
Efforts of the West University Neighborhood Association resulted in the creation of this open spot in the middle of the University and Hospital districts. This place reflects a trend toward the development of small, scattered neighborhood parks and away from large central parks. The pavillion and trellis provide modest cover along two sides and encourage flexible use of both open and covered spaces. Wood construction, brickwork and paving were done by a mix of students, professional contractors and volunteers.

19 CALKINS HOUSE 1902
588 E. 11th Avenue (NRHP)
1977 Restoration: Albert Pastine, architect
This large Queen Anne Style residence is perhaps the best of several large early houses built along 11th Avenue, the turn-of-the-century link between the University and the town. Its owner, W.W. Calkins, was a successful Eugene banker.

21 MARIAN HALL 1964
650 E. 11th Avenue
Wilmsen, Endicott & Unthank, architects
James S. Hickey, Inc., builder
This dormitory for Northwest Christian College uses its setback space as a buffer zone against the noisy street. Recessed a half-story below grade, courtyards provide private outdoor space and decrease the apparent building height. Sculptured concrete wall panels are by James Lee Hansen.

E. FAIRMOUNT

Fairmount began in 1890 as real estate developer George Melvin Miller's grand plan to found a new city between Eugene and Springfield. The first plat included the area extending from Agate Street to the lower slopes of the hills east of Fairmount Boulevard, between the Millrace and about 21st Avenue.

In addition to a luxurious residential area next to the University, Miller's plan included industrial development to be served by a railroad and depot. Only the residential development succeeded, and Miller's new town was finally annexed to Eugene about 1905; only then did growth begin east of Fairmount Boulevard. In 1906, part of the hillside was set aside as Hendricks Park.

Building surged in the 1920s and 1930s along the base of the hills and, in a few instances, at the top. Later years brought further development of the hillside sites, prized for their view of the University and the city.

The scene above Fairmount Boulevard is now one of a diversity of styles, from early cottages and bungalows to the most modern, all mixed informally on generous sites amid established landscaping.

Miller's own house, built around 1891, still stands at 1825 Fairmount Boulevard, although it has been extensively altered and enlarged.

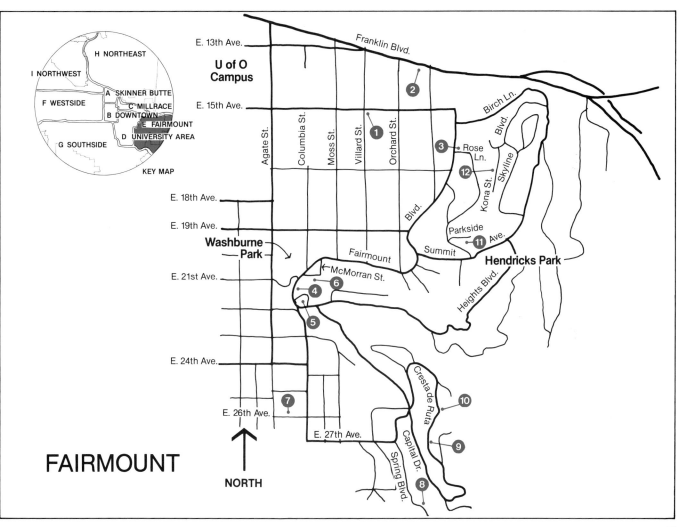

U of O Campus

KEY MAP

H NORTHEAST
I NORTHWEST
F WESTSIDE
A SKINNER BUTTE
C MILLRACE
B DOWNTOWN
E FAIRMOUNT
D UNIVERSITY AREA
G SOUTHSIDE

E. 13th Ave.
Franklin Blvd.
E. 15th Ave.
E. 18th Ave.
E. 19th Ave.
E. 21st Ave.
E. 24th Ave.
E. 26th Ave.
E. 27th Ave.

Agate St.
Columbia St.
Moss St.
Villard St.
Orchard St.

Birch Ln.
Blvd.
Rose Ln.
Kona St.
Skyline

Washburne Park

Fairmount
McMorran St.
Summit
Parkside
Ave.
Hendricks Park
Heights Blvd.

Cresta de Ruta
Capital Dr.
Spring Blvd.

FAIRMOUNT

NORTH

1 FAIRMOUNT PRESBYTERIAN CHURCH 1895
now the MAUDE KERNS ART CENTER
1910 E. 15th Avenue

This building, designed in a simplified, vernacular version of the Georgian Style, is the oldest church structure remaining in Eugene. It was later remodeled and enlarged to provide studios and gallery space for the Art Center.

2 JOE ROMANIA DISPLAY PAVILION 1959
2020 Franklin Boulevard
Balzhiser, Seder & Rhodes, architects
Gale M. Roberts Co., builder

Intended as an unobtrusive shelter for the automobiles on display, its curved form suggests the dynamism of the auto in motion and serves to focus attention on the product it contains. The roof form was conceived as a tension structure suspended from a perimeter compression ring but was built with conventional methods.

3 MORRIS HOUSE 1931
1669 Fairmount Boulevard
W.R.B. Willcox, architect
Arnt Ree, builder

One of Willcox's simplest and most direct designs emphasizes Morris' study in the large projecting bay.

5 WILSON H. JEWETT HOUSE 1921
2465 Fairmount Boulevard

Built to adjoin the Washburne house, this grand Colonial Revival style house shared its extensive grounds and garden. Jewett, a Eugene lumberman, was Mrs. Washburne's brother.

4 CARL WASHBURNE HOUSE c. 1920
2425 Fairmount Boulevard

This 17 room Colonial Revival Style house was once a part of a large estate that included the Wilson H. Jewett house and a large private garden which is now the Minnie L. Washburne Memorial Park. Washburne owned a department store with George McMorran.

6 McMORRAN HOUSE c. 1925
2315 McMorran Street
Roscoe Hemenway, architect

Now owned by the University of Oregon as a residence for its president, this imposing house combines several features of the Norman Farmhouse and English Tudor styles in its steep hip roofs, leaded glass, cut-stone entrance and the brick patterns of its front walls and chimneys.

CUSTOM-DESIGNED HOUSES

Each house in this collection is a custom design of highly individual appearance, yet all share a common basis in the design process. Particular attention has been given to the special demands and opportunities of its site and to organizing the spaces of the house around the individual needs and lifestyle of the family for whom it was designed. Still, its outward expression—the sum of its form, materials and detail—is the distinctive product of the architect's concept, carried out with unity and consistency.

8 OREM HOUSE   1978
2819 Spring Boulevard
Edward Waterbury, architect
Hayward-Flato Contractors, builders

9 MENTION HOUSE   1967
2695 Cresta de Ruta
Robert Mention, architect
Lyman Windheim, builder

7 HACKER HOUSE   1976
1665 E. 26th Avenue
Thom Hacker, designer, builder

10 TROMBLEY HOUSE 1965
2635 Cresta de Ruta
Otto Poticha, architect

12 HARRIS HOUSE 1969
1750 Kona Street
Robert S. Harris, architect
Gordon Wild, builder

11 SMITH HOUSE 1979
2300 Parkside Lane
Unthank Seder Poticha Architects
Clearview Const. Co., builder

F. WESTSIDE

The area immediately west of downtown and north of 11th Avenue has been prominent as a residential district from its beginning. The Blair Land Claim saw its first houses in the 1850s, but the railroad stimulated real growth in the 1880s and 1890s when it brought new residents in need of housing. The Westside was most prominent in this period as the site of construction of Eugene's largest and most stylistically articulate residences. As in other areas, some houses were moved here from earlier sites downtown.

Many of the original houses were replaced during a new building boom beginning about 1910 when a second generation of house building, this time in the predominant Bungalow Style, swept the area. Most of the houses in the Westside today belong to this period, but the rows of mature shade trees that line the streets stand as the major legacy of the earlier residents.

The prominence of the Westside declined as residential areas formed elsewhere, and its location next to the growing central business district put its future in question. In 1972 the question became academic when the neighborhood was split by the Washington-Jefferson Street Bridge.

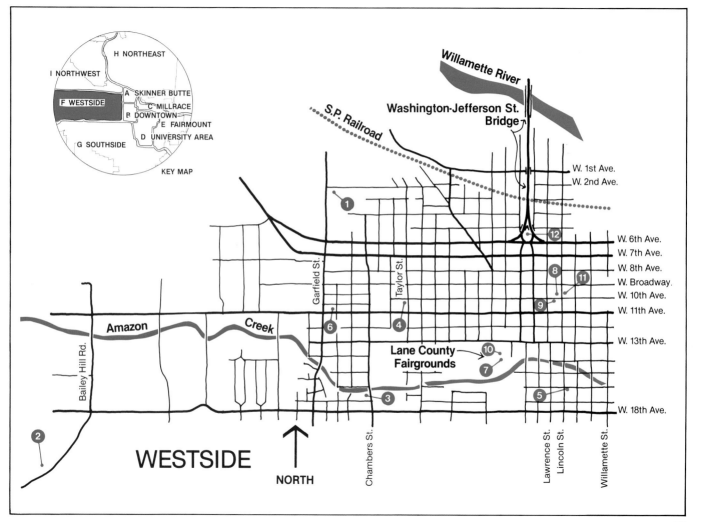

Key Map

H NORTHEAST
I NORTHWEST
A SKINNER BUTTE
C MILLRACE
F WESTSIDE
B DOWNTOWN
E FAIRMOUNT
D UNIVERSITY AREA
G SOUTHSIDE

KEY MAP

Willamette River

S.P. Railroad

Washington-Jefferson St. Bridge

W. 1st Ave.
W. 2nd Ave.
W. 6th Ave.
W. 7th Ave.
W. 8th Ave.
W. Broadway
W. 10th Ave.
W. 11th Ave.
W. 13th Ave.
W. 18th Ave.

Garfield St.
Taylor St.
Chambers St.
Lawrence St.
Lincoln St.
Willamette St.
Bailey Hill Rd.

Amazon   Creek

Lane County Fairgrounds

WESTSIDE

NORTH

67

WESTSIDE RESIDENCES

The area that lies generally west of Washington Street and extending from 11th Avenue to the parkland along the Willamette River has seen relatively little change since 1920-30 when residential development shifted to the University area and other perimeter locations. A few of the earliest 19th century houses remain with Classical Revival and Queen Anne detail but the area is best known for its numerous Bungalow Style residences, many of which replaced earlier houses. The features and rich detail that remain from each of these periods, set along the tree-lined streets of this neighborhood, make this one of the best walking or biking tours in Eugene.

3 WESTMORELAND MEDICAL-DENTAL CLINIC 1965

1650 Chambers Street
Wilmsen, Endicott & Unthank, architects
Gale M. Roberts Co., builder

Connected by covered walkways, the complex has been carefully sited to preserve an existing grove of oak trees.

1 CUDDEBACK LUMBER CO. DRYING SHEDS, YARD & BURNER

W. 2nd Avenue & Garfield Street

The collection of drying sheds, burners (now inactive), log decks and various buildings that have grown with the lumber industry has produced an architecture all its own. And when the processes of industry are as visible as they are here, the architecture of building and machine, organizing energy and motion, can become unusually dynamic.

2 JOHN F. KENNEDY JR. HIGH SCHOOL 1965

2200 Bailey Hill Road
Wilmsen, Endicott & Unthank, architects
Vik Construction Co., builder

Broad, sloping roofs with deep overhangs diminish the scale of the large building masses while providing sheltered passage between buildings in this campus-plan school. Long roof spans were made with folded plates—three-dimensional plywood beams fabricated on-site, which are seen as the repeating triangular forms on the roof.

4 **FRANK CHAMBERS HOUSE 1892**
1006 Taylor Street
Originally located at Broadway and Lincoln, this
house contains much of the ornamental woodwork
so distinctive in the Queen Anne houses remaining
today. It was built for Frank Chambers, a young
hardware merchant who helped establish the
Eugene Woolen Mill, Eugene Opera House and the
Y.M.C.A.

6 THE INDOOR GARDEN 1979
1915 W. 11th Avenue
The Amundsen Associates, architects
John Pratt, builder

Once an auto parts store, this conversion to a plant shop takes advantage of its existing orientation to both sun and highway to communicate its new functions. Such adaptive reuses can capitalize on many existing structures, revitalizing them and extending their useful lifespans.

5 PETERS-LISTON-WINTERMEIER HOUSE 1869,70
1611 Lincoln Street

A.V. Peters, a merchant, built this house at the southwest corner of Tenth and Pearl. It was moved here along with its stable in 1914. This is one of Oregon's finest examples of the Rural Gothic Style and features vertical board-and-batten siding, scrollwork balcony detail and bracketed eaves supporting steep roofs. The design appears to have been taken directly from an 1856 pattern book, except the plan was reversed.

7 **LANE COUNTY CONVENTION CENTER** 1980
Lane County Fairgrounds
W. 13th Avenue & Monroe Street
Wm. W. Wilson and Assoc., architects
Gale M. Roberts Co., builder
Column-free interiors, a flexible wall system and underfloor access permit adaptation of the large spaces into a number of interior configurations. Uses include trade shows, exhibitions, conventions, equestrian events and concerts.

8 **LINCOLN TERRACE HOUSES** 1980
W. 10th Avenue & Lincoln Street
Unthank Seder Poticha Architects
P.L.H. Thompson, landscape architect
R.A. Chambers Construction Co., builder
This project is significant for Eugene as one of the first examples of high-density housing in the central area. Parking is provided partly underground with housing units above organized around a central terraced courtyard. Exterior materials are simple and inexpensive but used in a sensitive way.

10 LANE COUNTY CLERK'S OFFICE 1853
Lane County Museum
740 W. 13th Avenue
Prior Blair, builder
This tiny, sturdy building is one of the oldest
remaining public buildings in Oregon and indicates
the scale of early county government. Its details are
naive in design if not in workmanship, but it captures the effect of a pedimented temple in the
Greek Revival Style. The building is believed to have
been originally located in the southwest corner of
the Park Blocks.

9 HIRAM SMEED HOUSE c. 1892
388 W. 10th Avenue
This simplified example of the Gothic Revival Style,
with its complex composition of wings and roofs,
also contains elements of the Stick Style in such
detail as the gable ornamentation and sawtooth vertical boarding in the bay windows.

11 THE OREGON BANK   1963
   10th and Lincoln Branch
Balzhiser, Seder & Rhodes, architects
Vik Const. Co., builder
This building emphasizes its pre-cast concrete structural system as its main organizing force. The perimeter columns are connected to concrete T-beams, forming a column-free space.

12 WASHINGTON-JEFFERSON STREET BRIDGE
   PARK   1974
Washington St. from 1st to 7th Avenues
Eugene Parks Dept., landscape designers
Paul Bros. Construction Co., builders
Sculpture by Bruce Beasley
Grassy open space, sculpture, trees and athletic courts are well planned to make the most of a modern urban problem—new freeways in old neighborhoods. Often filled or neglected, the leftover spaces created by this freeway overpass provide open space and recreation for inner-city neighborhoods.

G. SOUTHSIDE

In 1856, the Presbyterian church established Columbia College in a building on 19th Avenue between Olive and Charnelton. Like the first building at the University of Oregon twenty years later, it stood on a dry rise well away from the new town then known as Eugene City. Four years and two fires later, it closed. But the name College Hill remains.

A few houses were built near the college on the hill, and more were built there between 1900 and the Great Depression, when the city growth had extended farther south.

Growth was slow in the flatland between the hills south of 19th Avenue, because of wet ground and frequent flooding along Amazon Creek. The parklands that extend south to 30th Avenue were developed from the farsighted acquisition of this "unusable" land by the city in the 1940s.

The postwar period brought pressure for new development on a large scale, although material shortages slowed the housing boom somewhat. In the 1950s development accelerated south of the park, particularly after 1958 when the Amazon Slough was built to drain the area.

Today, the tracts of housing that filled the flats are reaching up the hillsides— now in the form of planned unit developments, condominiums and other multiple-family housing as land becomes limited by its form and by the urban services boundary.

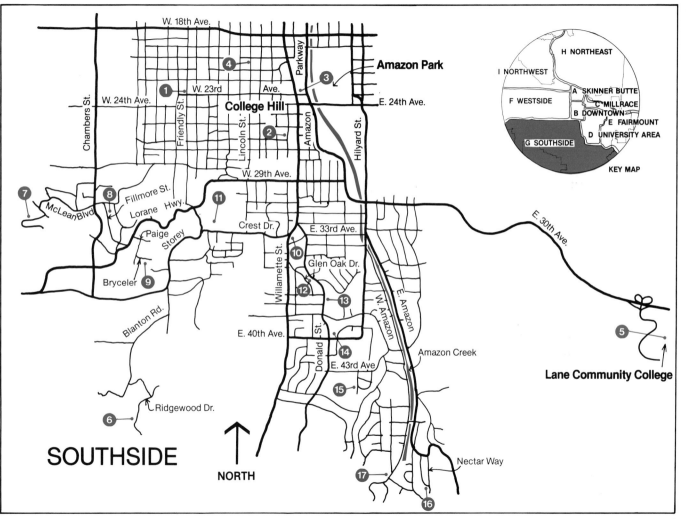

SOUTHSIDE

NORTH

Amazon Park

College Hill

W. 18th Ave.

W. 23rd

Ave.

W. 24th Ave.

E. 24th Ave.

W. 29th Ave.

Crest Dr.

E. 33rd Ave.

Glen Oak Dr.

E. 40th Ave.

E. 43rd Ave

Amazon Creek

Nectar Way

Lane Community College

Chambers St.

Friendly St.

Lincoln St.

Parkway

Amazon

Hilyard St.

Fillmore St.

McLean Blvd.

Lorane Hwy.

Paige

Storey

Bryceler

Blanton Rd.

Ridgewood Dr.

Willamette St.

Donald St.

W. Amazon

E. Amazon

E. 30th Ave.

KEY MAP

H NORTHEAST

I NORTHWEST

F WESTSIDE

A SKINNER BUTTE

C MILLRACE

B DOWNTOWN

E FAIRMOUNT

D UNIVERSITY AREA

G SOUTHSIDE

3 PARKWAY WILLAMETTE PROFESSIONAL
CENTER 1971
E. 23rd Avenue & Willamette Street
Unthank Seder Poticha Architects
Lloyd Bond, landscape architect
Gale M. Roberts Co., builder
This is a complex of individual buildings housing independent medical and dental practices. The gently sloping site and careful inter-relationship between the interior and exterior spaces gives a pleasant, non-clinical feeling to the various offices.

1 FRIENDLY STREET CHURCH OF GOD 1951
W. 23rd Avenue & Friendly Street
John Stafford, architect
Elson Shields, builder
This church is a fine composition of form and detail that clearly distinguishes between its church, school and social areas. Its irregular massing and mixed scales allow it to fit comfortably among the surrounding houses while still providing a focal point for the neighborhood.

2 TEMPLE BETH ISRAEL 1953
2550 Portland Street
H.H. Waechter, architect
Waldo Hardie & Son, builders
The main spaces of this building are organized around an interior courtyard which provides light and view while maintaining privacy. All artwork was executed by the architect. Of particular interest is the painting on the boxed plywood roof beams which can be seen from the courtyard.

5 LANE COMMUNITY COLLEGE CAMPUS 1968-69

4000 E. 30th Ave.
Balzhiser, Seder & Rhodes, architects
Mitchell & McArthur, landscape architects
1974 Theater by Unthank Seder Poticha
Architects
Various contractors

Many complete community college campuses were designed and constructed during the 1960s and 1970s. Unlike traditional campuses that grow slowly by accretion, these new community-oriented colleges are many times created as a whole. LCC was designed as a commuter campus and the separation of foot traffic from automobiles is a major design consideration. Because of its location far from existing community support services, LCC provides a mixture of classrooms, offices, shops, libraries, stores, etc., in an attempt to create its own community.

4 LANSDOWNE HOUSE 1890s
2056 Lincoln Street

The richly carved woodwork such as that preserved in this house was one of the chief hallmarks of the Queen Anne Style. While it was often fabricated by a local mill, stock pieces could also be obtained, ready-made, from mail-order houses.

6 **FOGELSON HOUSE** c. 1959
298 Ridgewood Drive
Frank Lloyd Wright, architect
1974 Addn.: Unthank Seder Poticha Architects
George Downs, builder

Frank Lloyd Wright designed this house to be part of an exhibit, using the flat roof common to the Prairie Style houses of that era. It was built from plans sold and mailed to the original owners by Wright without the traditional personal contact and supervision usually associated with his works. It is one of the few Wright buildings in Oregon. The second floor is a later addition attempting to continue in the Wright style.

7 **SEDER HOUSE** 1955
2385 McLean Boulevard
Grant Seder, architect
Vik Const. Co., builder

Space is economically enclosed in this A-frame structure whose tall form is appropriate to the surrounding woods. A full-length skylight captures added light from the deeply shaded environment.

8 **UNRUH HOUSE** 1966
3225 Fillmore Street
Richard L. Unruh, architect
Lloyd Ecklund, builder

This house is organized around a two-story family room. The flat roofs and projecting planes, multi-level plan and extensive use of glass are all characteristic of the International Style.

9 DUNCAN HOUSE 1951
3288 Bryceler Park
Pietro Belluschi, architect
Warren Vale, builder

This is one of the earliest Eugene houses designed specifically with passive solar capabilities in mind. It was Belluschi's entry in a Libby Owens Ford passive solar house competition and was selected by the owner from a subsequent publication. Its passive solar characteristics include south-facing windows and concrete floors that store radiated solar heat.

10 DUPLEX 1980
3291 Willamette & 15 E. 33rd Avenue
Earl Moursund, architect
Craig Krimmel, builder

In this building, irregular, fragmented forms of stucco and wood are combined with a tile roof to produce a very personal character suggestive of the vernacular expressions found in old-world buildings.

11 WAYNE MORSE RANCH 1936
595 Crest Drive
Wallace Hayden, architect

Organized as a group of farm buildings, the ranch is now a city park. The main house was designed to have a commanding view of the southern Willamette Valley and to accommodate the family life of a U.S. Senator.

12 BRONN HOUSE 1950s
3585 Glen Oak Drive
Miller & Morton, designers and builders

These are two of about fifteen houses designed and
built by Miller and Morton between 1952 and 1957.
Six occur in a row between numbers 3565 and 3635
on the east side of Glen Oak Drive. Most were custom designs for owners in this part of Eugene.
Though individually different, their houses usually included large glass areas under broad, sheltering
roofs, extensive use of wood for both structure and
finish and siting seeming natural to the property—
characteristics now so associated with the Northwest that they have become part of the region's
vernacular.

13 BALLINGER HOUSE 1950s
3715 Donald Street
Miller & Morton, designers and builders

14 UNITARIAN CHURCH 1963
447 E. 40th Avenue
Balzhiser, Seder and Rhodes, architects
Don Furtick, builder

The lightweight exposed wood framing and extensive use of glass opens the building to the trees that
surround it. Most notable is the non-directional main
meeting space placed over the classroom spaces.

15 MARCZUK HOUSE
4430 Hilyard Street
Michael Marczuk, architect
Larson Bros. Const. Co., builders

By rotating the house 45° to the street and garage, the architect was able to make the entry to the house less abrupt and avoid the traditional front-back feeling of typical suburban houses. The house is notable for its simple geometric forms and refined style.

17 PEARL BUCK CENTER 1959
5100 W. Amazon Drive
H.H. Waechter, architect
Builders: Charles Lake (1959),
Howard Nelson (1967 Addn.)

This specialized facility supports a life-span program for the handicapped. The plan reflects the contours of the sloping wooded site with changes in levels made by interior ramps. The complex is of wood-frame construction except for the multi-purpose building which is of reinforced concrete with a pre-stressed concrete roof.

16 TIMBER VILLAGE 1975-76
5200 block of Nectar Way
Morris & Redden, architects
Lloyd Bond, landscape architect
Al Summers, builder

This development of traditional townhouses on a steep hillside site offered some of the first multi-family residences in the hills surrounding Eugene. The small repeating gables identify each unit and reduce the overall scale of the building complex.

H. NORTHEAST

The predominantly residential area northeast of the river has spread through once-isolated farmlands over the same framework of roads that originally served these farms. Coburg Road in particular was an important early route of travel.

Development has only recently extended beyond Beltline Road. More has been proposed east of Coburg Road on the Cone-Breeden property (once the Armitage Farm).

Riverfront development is also quite recent. The construction of Highway I-105 helped to promote the development of Valley River Center, now an extensive core of retail stores attracting further growth to its edges. The center competes strongly with the downtown area for shopping supremacy in Eugene. The center is connected with Alton Baker Park by a network of bike trails that follow nearly undisturbed banks on both sides of the river. Jogging trails and a three-mile canoe course wander through the park whose east end was reclaimed from a sanitary landfill.

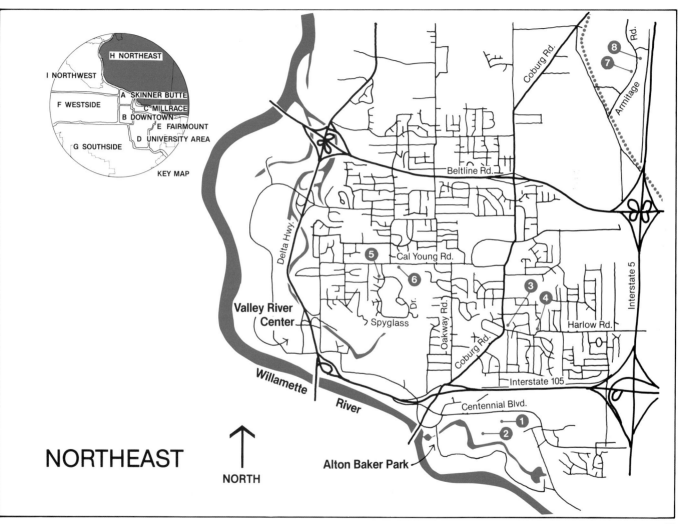

NORTHEAST

NORTH

KEY MAP

H NORTHEAST
I NORTHWEST
F WESTSIDE
A SKINNER BUTTE
C MILLRACE
B DOWNTOWN
E FAIRMOUNT
D UNIVERSITY AREA
G SOUTHSIDE

Coburg Rd.
Armitage Rd.
Beltline Rd.
Interstate 5
Delta Hwy.
Cal Young Rd.
Spyglass
Dr.
Oakway Rd.
Coburg Rd.
Harlow Rd.
Interstate 105
Centennial Blvd.
Valley River Center
Willamette River
Alton Baker Park

2 **PLANETARIUM AND MUSEUM 1979**
   Alton Baker Park
Lutes Sanetel Architects
J.E. Beck Co., builder
This building is the first of a three-building cultural
center planned for Alton Baker Park. Its severely
simple geometric forms suggest its dual function—
the cylindrical part of the building houses the Planetarium projector.

1 **AUTZEN STADIUM 1967**
   Centennial Boulevard
Skidmore, Owings and Merrill, architects
Gale M. Roberts Co., builder
With its perimeter built up from earth taken from the
surrounding site, this economical landfill stadium becomes more like a butte than a building. The simple
ramped circulation was designed to reduce the
mazelike confusion of so many similar facilities.

3 WESTMINSTER PRESBYTERIAN CHURCH 1961
777 Coburg Road
Stewart & Richardson, architects
Carleton Const. Co., builder

The understated exterior of barn-like forms and materials conceals a lively interior of curved forms and colorful surfaces. The sanctuary opens to enclosed exterior courtyards in a manner similar to Pietro Belluschi's designs of the previous decade.

4 ELMER HARLOW HOUSE 1922
2991 Harlow Road (NRHP)

This house is representative of the Bungalow Style with its low, horizontal mass, heavy posts and overhanging eaves. The use of brick construction is unusual.

5 CHAMPIGNON TOWNHOUSES AND URBAN COTTAGES 1979
Spyglass Drive
Threshold/ a group of architects
Peter L.H. Thompson, landscape architect
Spyglass Development, builders

This 66 unit project mixing row houses, urban cottages and single family residences is a careful blend of fine design and cultured nostalgia. Well-scaled spaces between buildings mixed with the feeling of the woods convey a sense of both independence and community.

6 CAL YOUNG HOUSE 1913
1610 Cal Young Road

Although extensively remodeled in 1928, the Cal Young house remains as a historic landmark to honor one of Lane County's first and leading families. Only the brick milk house remains from the 1913 building—the third house built on the site of Charles W. Young's 1852 land claim.

8 **GEORGE ARMITAGE HOUSE** c. 1855
now **JOHNSON'S VEGETABLE FARM**
89733 Armitage Road
George Armitage, builder

This house was originally built one-half mile south
on the Armitage Farm and moved here in 1918.
Beneath asbestos siding is one of Oregon's few
Palladian-form, Classical Style houses. On the back
of the house are some of the original sash windows
(six panes over six panes).

7 **GEORGE ARMITAGE FARM** 1851-1918
89618 Armitage Road

In recent years this site has lost many early buildings. Those remaining include the large Bungalow
Style house, 1918; the brick dairy near the house on
the north, c.1870; the garage (originally, the smoke
house), c. 1870; and behind the garage, the un-
painted wood granary (one of the few extant in Lane
County), c. 1860.

I. NORTHWEST

This part of the city has a history similar to that of the Northeast area, with one exception—it is the side with the railroad.

Historically, River Road was the main route connecting Eugene with towns to the north. Stages brought settlers to Eugene over this road until the railroad took over in 1871. Farms were developed on land claims along its length to Junction City, but urban development, spreading northward after 1900, removed nearly all traces of these farms south of Beltline along both River Road and its successor, U.S. Highway 99.

Lumber and other industries built their mills and warehouses along the railroad here and in the Westside after leaving earlier sites on the Millrace and on the south side of Skinner Butte.

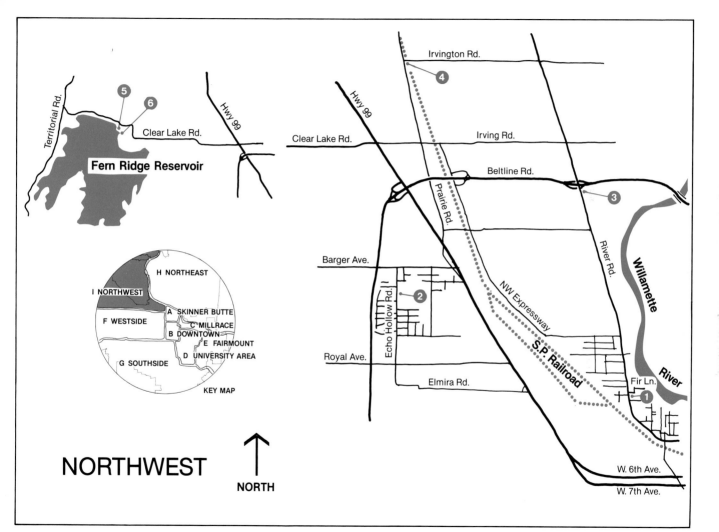

Territorial Rd.

Hwy 99

⑤ ⑥

Clear Lake Rd.

Fern Ridge Reservoir

H NORTHEAST

I NORTHWEST

F WESTSIDE

A SKINNER BUTTE

C MILLRACE

B DOWNTOWN

E FAIRMOUNT

D UNIVERSITY AREA

G SOUTHSIDE

KEY MAP

Irvington Rd.

④

Hwy 99

Clear Lake Rd.

Irving Rd.

Beltline Rd.

③

Prairie Rd.

River Rd.

Willamette

Barger Ave.

Echo Hollow Rd.

②

NW Expressway

S.P. Railroad

Royal Ave.

River

Elmira Rd.

Fir Ln.

①

NORTHWEST

↑

NORTH

W. 6th Ave.

W. 7th Ave.

1 **WALLACE POTTER HOUSE** **1929**
120 Fir Lane
Hunzicker & Smith, architects
Some of the best Tudor Revival architecture in
Eugene can be seen in this house and one across
the road—built in 1930 for another member of the
Potter family. Together, they reflect semi-rural living
in the early 20th century.

3 **RIVER ROAD TRANSIT STATION** **1982**
River Road at River Avenue
Lutes Sanetel Architects
Wildish Construction Co., builder
This project was the first of several "Park and Ride"
facilities intended as a convenient meeting ground
between mass transit and the suburban public.
Information signage is well integrated into the
shelters which were treated as open "umbrellas"
rather than as enclosed spaces out of concern for
full visibility and user security.

2 **ECHO HOLLOW SWIMMING POOL** **1969**
1655 Echo Hollow Road
Briscoe and Berry, architects
Leo Kowalewski, builder
This 50 meter indoor-outdoor pool can be converted
to a 25 yard indoor pool by means of a rolling wall
and a submersible concrete pool divider. This divider
is recessed into the bottom of the pool when it is
used as a 50 meter open pool in the summer, and is
raised in the winter to confine the heated, indoor
pool area.

4 UNITED BRETHREN CHURCH 1891
Since 1942 the IRVING CHRISTIAN
CHURCH
90341 Prairie Road
A polygonal vestibule roofed with a pyramidal
steeple gives distinction and a German Romanesque
character to this white shiplap country church. The
photograph shows this remarkably intact landmark
in its original Prairie Road location. However it is
being relocated to adjoin new facilities in the 1300
block of Irvington Drive.

6 FOOTBRIDGE 1965
Orchard Point, Fern Ridge Reservoir
John L. Briscoe, architect
Lane County Public Works Dept., builder
This footbridge forms part of a lakefront path sys-
tem and divides a wading pond from the deeper
lake. It is built of wood using simple metal con-
nectors.

5 CONCESSIONS BUILDINGS &
SHELTERS 1963-65
Orchard Point County Park, Fern Ridge Reservoir
Phil Gilmore, architect
Builders: Ed Lackey (1963), Army Engineers (1965)
These structures were designed to mark the park
entrance and form a relationship between the park
and the reservoir without competing with its natural
surroundings for dominance.

SPRINGFIELD

Springfield's development as an industrial center provides a sharp contrast to its partner across the Willamette River, Eugene. It was settled by Elias and Mary Briggs in 1848 on a donation land claim situated between the McKenzie and Willamette rivers, a rich prairie suitable for agriculture and surrounded by virgin timber. The two rivers provided the abundant waterpower then necessary for the beginning of a strong industrial community.

Briggs began a millrace on the Willamette in 1852 to power the first flour and sawmills in 1853-54. These two industries set the stage for the economic development of the town that is now the second most important industrial center in the state.

The first plat, in 1856, consisted of the two blocks between South A, Main, Mill and Third streets. Activity centered on Mill Street along the river; with its two mills, the town was expected to grow and flourish as an industrial center. Despite its promising setting, Springfield grew slowly. The river was navigable to Springfield only during floods, and without reliable river transportation markets were on the whole inaccessible. The real blow, though, fell in 1871, when the main line of the Oregon and California Railroad was routed to Eugene. Springfield's population declined from 649 in 1860 to 371 in 1890.

In 1891, the city finally gained a railroad line and growth resumed. The major activity moved from Mill to Main Street, which paralleled the railroad. The flour mill was renovated and the Booth-Kelly Lumber Co. built its mills at the south end of town.

The main residential area of that time is still intact today. It grew from Mill Street to what is about 10th Street and from South A to F or G, extending eastward from the river and northward from the mills and railroad. Beyond 10th Street were the prairies and timberlands that provided a convenient source of food and raw materials. The rivers and railroad provided access to other timber lands, solidifying the economic base of the community.

Lifestyle and residential patterns were affected by the industries. Booth-Kelly employees were often called to work and live at various logging camps. Through these camps, the towns of Wendling, Marcola and Mabel that lie to the northeast became intertwined with the history of Springfield. Railroad spurs connected these towns to their major population resource in Springfield. Residents migrated between logging camps and farms to earn a living—a characteristic that shaped the early economy and the character of the city.

Growth accelerated after World War II. In 1940, the city's population was 3,800 within an area of 1.5 square miles, compared to 42,000 people and 12 square miles in 1980. The residential area, once clustered north of downtown, expanded to the north and east. Industry expanded eastward along the southern edge but the absence of planned development brought problems. Old mills mingled with residences and the street systems lacked thoroughfares between residential, commercial and industrial areas. As residential areas moved outward and competition from Eugene increased, retailing declined downtown.

Several efforts were made to revitalize the downtown area and give order to expansion. In 1956-57, Springfield undertook the Third Street Urban Renewal Project, demolishing blighted houses and industries, and redeveloping the area with street paving, lights and sidewalks. In 1957, Main Street was converted to a pedestrian mall on a trial basis. Although sales increased and shoppers approved, a permanent conversion was not made. A 1968 Springfield Core Area Plan again attempted to reroute major traffic and discourage the automobile in the central core, but again the plan was abandoned.

In recent years, competition from suburban shopping centers has stripped the central core of many of its retailers and, along with them, its role as Springfield's primary shopping area. While the downtown is left to find new purpose, more recent commercial and residential development pushes to the north and east in search of ultimate boundaries. It is a pattern familiar to many cities—one that raises important questions of land use, extended urban services and, ultimately, cohesive city identity.

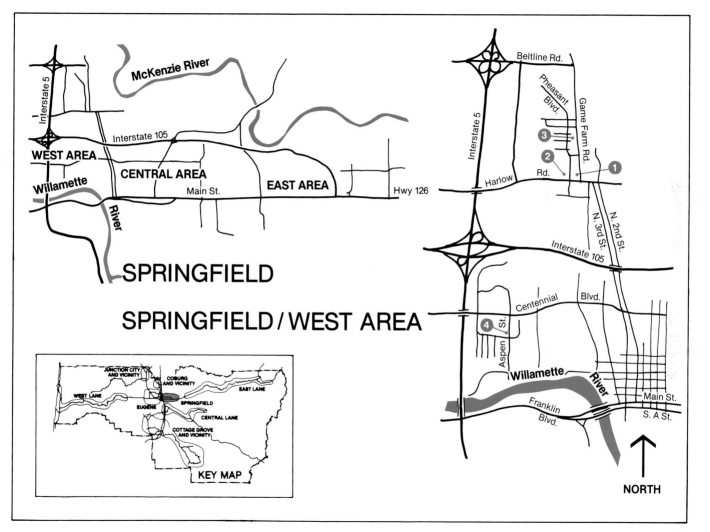

McKenzie River

Interstate 5

Interstate 105

WEST AREA

CENTRAL AREA

EAST AREA

Willamette

River

Main St.

Hwy 126

SPRINGFIELD

SPRINGFIELD / WEST AREA

Beltline Rd.

Pheasant Blvd.

Game Farm Rd.

Interstate 5

Harlow Rd.

N. 3rd St.

N. 2nd St.

Interstate 105

Centennial Blvd.

Aspen St.

Willamette River

Main St.

Franklin Blvd.

S. A St.

NORTH

KEY MAP

JUNCTION CITY AND VICINITY

COBURG AND VICINITY

WEST LANE

EAST LANE

EUGENE

SPRINGFIELD

CENTRAL LANE

COTTAGE GROVE AND VICINITY

1 JAMES STEVENS HOUSE 1875
2638 Game Farm Road

This is a second-generation home located on the land claim of William Stevens, whose house still stands nearby. Its roof shapes were typical of modified Gothic Revival Style houses. The exceptional brickwork of hearts and diamonds motifs in the main chimney, seen here and in the Campbell house, suggests the work of Rev. Charles Hamilton Wallace.

2 GAS STATION c. 1960
Harlow Road & Pheasant Boulevard
Balzhiser, Seder & Rhodes, architects

Here is a striking example from a brief period when building form was derived directly from unique structural forms and concepts. The hyperbolic-paraboloid roof transfers its stresses through the curved plane of the roof to the concrete abutments at the corners. The structure was originally designed and used as a gas station.

3 WILLIAM STEVENS HOUSE 1851
3050 Game Farm Road

This is possibly the oldest house in Lane County, one of about eight from the 1850s and the only two-story example. The house is partly obscured by the 1957 Baptist Church addition but survives with such fine period detail as the acorn pattern at the eaves. William Stevens' 1847 claim was the first in this area.

4 ROBERT E. CAMPBELL HOUSE 1873
890 Aspen Street (NRHP)

Once a farmhouse, this popular version of the Rural Gothic Style remains reasonably intact in form and detail from Campbell's 1851 D.L.C. Though modified with horizontal siding, gothic detailing can be seen in the tall second floor window (built as a glazed door opening onto the porch roof), in the organic motifs carried out in the jigsaw work and in the interior woodwork.

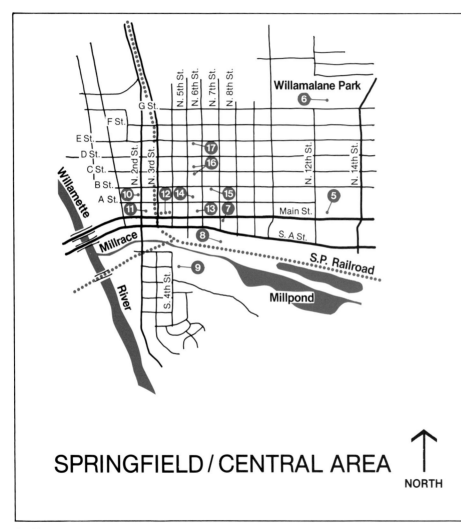

SPRINGFIELD / CENTRAL AREA

NORTH

Willamalane Park

Willamette River

Millrace

Millpond

S.P. Railroad

G St.
F St.
E St.
D St.
C St.
B St.
A St.
Main St.
S. A St.

N. 2nd St.
N. 3rd St.
N. 5th St.
N. 6th St.
N. 7th St.
N. 8th St.
N. 12th St.
N. 14th St.
S. 4th St.

5 **BRATTAIN/HADLEY HOUSE** **1893**
1260 Main Street
John B. Innis, builder
John Evans, mason

This is one of Springfield's oldest surviving houses and is representative of the Queen Anne Style. Of unusual quality are the decorative patterning on the surface of the house, the design of supports in the bays and the original foundation of fractured black basalt. With the exception of a closed back porch built in 1913, the exterior has not been altered.

6 WILLAMALANE POOL   1963
1276 G Street
Lutes & Amundsen, architects
Carleton Construction Co., builder

At the time of its construction, the Lamella roof—a vaulted form of intersecting arches—spanned further than any of this type ever built in wood. Its unencumbered volume is light and spacious, relieving the sense of indoor enclosure.

8 SOUTHERN PACIFIC DEPOT   1891
South end of 7th Street

This depot is the only commercial structure of its type in Springfield and the oldest depot of its type in Oregon. It is a long, rectangular wood-frame structure with a small, second story attached on its west end. It boasts several exterior textures: horizontal shiplap, a band of lath on the second story and imbricated shingling.

7 EQUITABLE SAVINGS & LOAN   1966
707 Main Street
Wilmsen, Endicott & Unthank, architects
W.E. Youel Const. Co., builder

The abrupt, steep form of the roof is a bold statement that terminates a block of simple buildings with the power of an exclamation point.

10 STEWART HOUSE 1906
214 2nd Street
Edgar Collins, builder

This house, built for the son of an early pioneer, lies on the site of the original Elias Briggs land claim and next to the spring that gave the city its name. It was a prominent residence in the youthful community. The varied treatment of the windows illustrates characteristic features such as the lattice pattern in the upper sashes. At one side is the original porte cochere.

11 BELL THEATER 1910
212-16 Main Street
J.A. Seaney, builder

This sandy brick two-story commercial structure has accommodated many uses over its lifetime: the second story, relatively unaltered, has housed apartments, but the ground floor, whose facade has been greatly altered, has housed (often on a shared basis) theaters (including the original), a clothing store, a restaurant and a furniture store. The whole facade is topped by a projecting wooden cornice.

9 TOMSETH HOUSE 1910
309 S. 4th Street

The exterior of this two and one-half story house contains classical features that remain significantly unaltered except for its new concrete block foundation and the addition of a concrete back porch. One-and-one-half-plank entablatures encircle the house both under the eaves and between ground and second stories.

12 SPRINGFIELD ARMORY 1921
326 Main Street
STEVENS-PERKINS BUILDING 1911
330 Main Street
George W. Perkins, probable builder
I.O.O.F. BUILDING 1907
342 Main Street

This trio of adjoining, commercial, two-story, masonry structures contains only one unchanging use among them; that of the second floor of the I.O.O.F. Building which has been used continuously by the Oddfellows Lodge since the building's construction. The Springfield Armory with its common bond brick and large arched entrance is the plainest of the three. The Stevens-Perkins Building with its tan common bond brick has panels of small white and brown patterned tiles between second story windows and a facade topped by a stepped false front. The I.O.O.F. Building of stucco-faced brick is classically detailed.

13 PACIFIC POWER AND LIGHT 1908
now the SPRINGFIELD MUSEUM
550 Main Street

This design prototype for Oregon Power Company electrical substations is associated with the advent of electrical power in Springfield. Now used as a museum, the building is notable for its carefully crafted detailing in brick and cast stone. Though the one-story front was heavily altered in the 1940s or 1950s, the two-story portion remains a striking use of classical composition.

15 INNIS HOUSE 1910
637 B Street
John B. Innis, builder

This one-and-one-half-story Queen Anne Style house, built by a master carpenter, boasts a bay window, steep roof pitch, brackets, diagonal pattern shingles and decorative trim on the eaves, gables and cornices. The back porch was partially replaced by a garage after 1912.

14 CITY HALL & LIBRARY 1975, 1981
225 N. 5th Street
1975 Building: Mike Rosenberg, architect
J.E. Beck Co., builder
1981 Conversion: Lutes Sanetel Architects
J.E. Beck Co., builder

This structure was originally built as an elevated downtown shopping center that proved commercially unsuccessful. The city recognized in it an opportunity both to gain needed space for administrative offices and library and to convert a public liability into a civic asset in the same stroke. Now its remodeled interior "streets" wind between blocks of offices in a structure that has become a "shopping center" for city services.

17 **REV. MOORE HOUSE** **1927**
535 E Street
This elegant two-story Bungalow Style house is
sided with stucco and encased on the front and side
by a wide, L-shaped porch. The front door and
windows facing onto the porch contain beveled
glass. The interior also contains much of its original
fine detailing.

16 **EBBERT MEMORIAL CHURCH** **1916**
525 C Street
A.I. Crandall, architect
McCracken, Male, builders
Stained glass by the Povey Brothers
EBBERT MEMORIAL PARSONAGE **1916**
530 C Street
McCracken, Male, builders
Constructed of stone in a Romanesque or Richard-
sonian Style, this Methodist Church retains many
original details including large, colorful stained glass
windows, some leaded glass and some painted
glass. Although changes to the interior have
affected the altar and have reduced the nave aisles
from three to two, the pews are original. The simple
lines of the wood-frame parsonage are accented by
heavy detailing in the window trim.

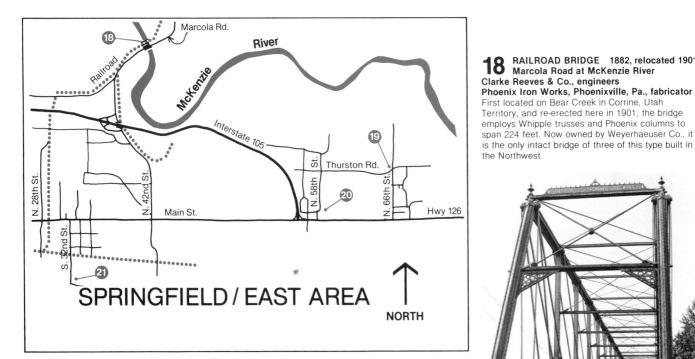

SPRINGFIELD / EAST AREA

NORTH

18 RAILROAD BRIDGE   1882, relocated 1901
Marcola Road at McKenzie River
Clarke Reeves & Co., engineers
Phoenix Iron Works, Phoenixville, Pa., fabricator
First located on Bear Creek in Corrine, Utah Territory, and re-erected here in 1901, the bridge employs Whipple trusses and Phoenix columns to span 224 feet. Now owned by Weyerhaeuser Co., it is the only intact bridge of three of this type built in the Northwest.

19 THURSTON COMMUNITY HALL   1913
66th Street and Thurston Road
Morris Brown, designer
Townspeople helped to build this structure which originally served as a meeting hall for community social functions. The arched ceiling was modeled on that of a Salem tabernacle. The interior has been remodeled with the addition of a kitchen and a full second story.

21 **DOUGLAS HOUSE**   **1908**
961 S. 32nd Street
John Hunzicker, architect

This house, one of the most ornate in Springfield, incorporates features from several styles. A Federal Style porch fronts the ground floor while Italianate detailing ornaments the second floor. The third floor facade contains a Palladian window below a Greek Revival broken pediment. Only minor changes have altered the interior and exterior.

20 **THURSTON HIGH SCHOOL**   **1961**
333 N. 58th Street
Wilmsen & Endicott, architects
Waldo S. Hardie & Son, builders

This campus-plan school was formed with its building units arranged in checkerboard fashion allowing expansion by infill in recent years. Its simple exterior treatment provides a strong sense of unity to the varied elements of the building complex.

COBURG & VICINITY

Like several other small communities in the Willamette Valley, time has not brought dramatic change to the character of Coburg, and many of its early buildings still exist.

Coburg was settled by John Diamond and Jacob Spores in 1847. The town stands on Diamond's land claim, later sold to Isaac Van Duyn whose house at 238 W. Van Duyn may be the oldest surviving building in Lane County. Another house of the Van Duyn family, built in 1877, is now the Coburg Inn. Spores claimed land to the south near the present Armitage Bridge and established an important ferry crossing there along the east Territorial Road. His house also remains—another of the earliest buildings still standing in Lane County.

The first cabin recorded in the county was erected near here at the confluence of the McKenzie and Willamette rivers by Donald McKenzie about 1814; not a permanent home, the cabin was used as a trading post by trappers and traders of the Hudson's Bay Co.

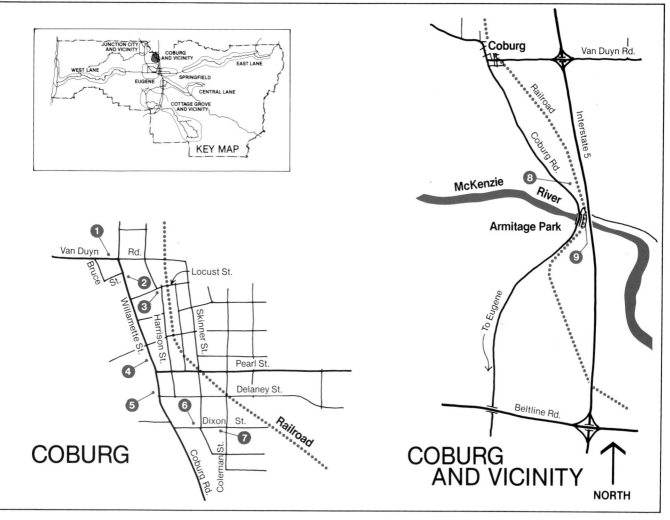

KEY MAP

JUNCTION CITY AND VICINITY

COBURG AND VICINITY

WEST LANE

EAST LANE

EUGENE

SPRINGFIELD

CENTRAL LANE

COTTAGE GROVE AND VICINITY

COBURG

Van Duyn Rd.

Bruce St.

Willamette St.

Harrison St.

Locust St.

Skinner St.

Pearl St.

Delaney St.

Dixon St.

Coleman St.

Coburg Rd.

Railroad

Coburg

Van Duyn Rd.

Railroad

Coburg Rd.

Interstate 5

McKenzie River

Armitage Park

To Eugene

Beltline Rd.

COBURG AND VICINITY

NORTH

1 ISAAC VAN DUYN—VAN MASSEY HOUSE   c.1850
238 W. Van Duyn

Family records indicate that the one-story wing was constructed as early as 1848, which would make it the oldest building remaining in Lane County. The addition of a two-story wing with characteristics from about 1870 gave the building a vernacular Gothic Revival appearance through its vertical form and T-shaped mass. Exterior detail is obscured by the later addition of asbestos siding.

2 GOODALE-JARNIGAN HOUSE   1878
444 N. Willamette Street

This large, two-story house was built for Goodale who owned the local lumber mill. The exterior contains simplified Italianate detail such as that seen in the pedimented window heads. The porch was replaced after 1900 in the then-popular Bungalow Style.

3 **CROSS HOUSE** c.1900
145 E. Locust Street

This is a very good example of a small one-story house type still commonly found throughout Oregon. The square hip roof (occasionally terminated by a flat roof section) and the single pane over single pane sash suggest the Italianate Style, though its basic features are largely vernacular.

4 **VAN DUYN HOUSE** 1877
now the COBURG INN
209 N. Willamette Street

Although extensive interior changes have occurred in the first floor as a result of the structure's conversion to a restaurant, the upper exterior part, including the bracketed eaves and Italianate hip roof, remain intact. A fine brick chimney may be the work of mason C.H. Wallace.

5 POLLARD-HEACOCK HOUSE c.1855
163 S. Willamette Street

Set back from the street behind an old-fashioned garden, this one and a half story, "double" house is Federal in style although the eave returns in the gable ends are Classical Revival features. Attached at the rear is a large hand-hewn framed woodshed. Workmanship and detail are characteristic of the 1850s.

6 HAMLIN-GEORGE HOUSE 1909
248 E. Dixon

This is a handsome example of a design reflecting the transition in styles which occurred at this time. The predominant Queen Anne Style of the hip roof form contrasts with the Bungalow Style characteristics of the wraparound porch and attached gable roofs. Hamlin was superintendent of Coburg's Booth Kelly mill.

7 CHANDLER HOUSE 1907
355 E. Dixon

This house is unusual for its diminutive scale. A wealth of Queen Anne features remain intact in its wraparound porch, turned posts and imbricated shingle pattern. The details, rather late for this style, continue in the kitchen wing and shed.

8 JACOB SPORES HOUSE 1855
90311 Coburg Road (NRHP)
Restored 1975 by Gregg Olson
This early one and one-half story vernacular farmhouse is notable for its exceptional restoration. Missing elements of fine Classical Revival woodwork were accurately reproduced with hand tools to match the original.

9 SOUTHERN PACIFIC R.R. BRIDGE 1887, Relocated 1907
near Coburg Road at McKenzie River (NRHP)
Relocated by American Bridge Company
Originally fabricated in 1887 for Oregon Railway and Navigation Company and erected over the John Day River in central Oregon, this bridge was relocated here in 1907. It was designed with Pratt trusses made with pin-connected rolled iron members to span 405 feet.

JUNCTION CITY & VICINITY

Junction City was one of many valley communities that grew to serve its agricultural surroundings. Its name came from a planned railroad junction that never materialized (rather than from the junction of highways that was built later).

The community is well known for its Scandinavian population—encouraged in the early 1900s by A.C. Neilsen, who divided his 1,600-acre property into 40- to 60-acre parcels and offered them to Danes from the Midwest to settle in the area. The Danish, who brought their skills in agriculture, dairying and carpentry, were joined by Norwegian and Swedish settlers who developed the area's early lumber industry.

Junction City prospered because of its situation on the main valley highway until Interstate 5 was built well to the east and its vitality began to decline. Borrowing on its heritage, the Scandinavian Festival was created in 1961 to revitalize the community. Its great success brought new pride and identity to the community —now occasionally evident in new buildings and storefronts that have appropriated Scandinavian motifs to celebrate the theme. These stand in interesting contrast to many 19th-century buildings built by the Scandinavian settlers in the prevailing Willamette Valley styles of the time—with little reference to the ornament and styles of their homelands.

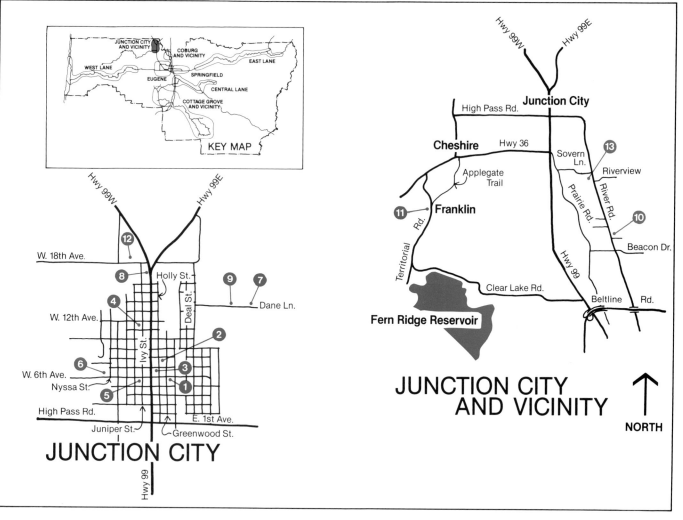

KEY MAP

JUNCTION CITY AND VICINITY
COBURG AND VICINITY
EAST LANE
WEST LANE
SPRINGFIELD
EUGENE
CENTRAL LANE
COTTAGE GROVE AND VICINITY

Hwy 99W
Hwy 99E
W. 18th Ave.
Holly St.
Deal St.
Dane Ln.
W. 12th Ave.
Ivy St.
W. 6th Ave.
Nyssa St.
High Pass Rd.
E. 1st Ave.
Juniper St.
Greenwood St.

JUNCTION CITY

Hwy 99

Hwy 99W
Hwy 99E
Junction City
High Pass Rd.
Cheshire
Hwy 36
Sovern Ln.
Applegate Trail
Riverview
Prairie Rd.
River Rd.
Franklin
Territorial Rd.
Beacon Dr.
Clear Lake Rd.
Hwy 99
Fern Ridge Reservoir
Beltline   Rd.

JUNCTION CITY AND VICINITY

NORTH

1 ODD FELLOWS LODGE 1909
590 Greenwood

This two-story structure with its simple classical entablature and formally placed openings is characteristic of early 20th century commercial buildings. Lodge rooms were located on the second floor. Junction City has a number of these early commercial buildings, including a few 19th century cast-iron fronts such as the one at 556 Greenwood.

2 HOUSE c.1870
789 Greenwood

Although some surface changes have been made, much fine Gothic Revival form and detail remains in the sharp, central gable roof and front entrance. The central chimney is exceptional brickwork in the Gothic Revival tradition.

3 DR. NORMAN LEE HOUSE c.1875
now the JUNCTION CITY MUSEUM
655 Holly Street (NRHP)

One of the oldest houses in Junction City is typical of two-story designs popular in the 1870s that combine Italianate features such as projecting window heads with such Gothic Revival detail as that of the porch post moldings. Lee was the first physician in the area.

4 **COL. FOLSOM HOUSE** c.1870
1187 Juniper Street

One of the most distinctive examples of the Italianate Style in Lane County, the Folsom house retains much of its original, excellent detailing in the low-pitched roof, bracketed eaves and classical window frames.

5 **P.N.B. TELEPHONE EQUIPMENT BLDG.**
1975
6th Avenue and Juniper Street
WEGROUP Architects
Quentin Greenough, Inc., builder

Conscious of its location among established residences, this unmanned equipment building combines deep setbacks, heavily landscaped yards and a fragmented building mass to soften its impact while remaining honest about its function.

6 **FAITH LUTHERAN CHURCH** 1906-08
926 6th Avenue
Mads Jensen, builder

This building is a center of much of the Scandinavian community in Junction City. Its steeply pitched multiple roof forms and entrance features vaguely recall the traditions of the Scandinavian stave churches, although its design probably borrowed more directly from the popular Gothic Revival period, then about over in this area.

8 CLIFFORD GAS STATION   c.1930
now THE BROWN JUG
1667 Ivy Street

Whether it is called Expressionist, Folk Art, Bizarre or Kitsch—there is always one building that is sure to tickle someone's fantasy.

9 A.C. NEILSEN HOUSE   c.1905
near 29321 Dane Lane

This unusual variation of the Queen Anne Style incorporates small gables that spring almost capriciously from each corner of a dominant, central hip roof. The horizontal banding of imbricated shingles over shiplap siding is more characteristic of Queen Anne detail.

7 SOREN JENSEN HOUSE   1904
29361 Dane Lane
Soren Jensen, builder

Jensen built a number of Junction City buildings from designs usually founded in the Queen Anne Style. In the case of his own house, the usually lively composition of Queen Anne elements is constrained by the formal, almost neo-Classical symmetry of the main facade.

10 THISTLE-DOWN FARM c.1910
91440 River Road

This complex of farm buildings is remarkable for its quality and unified design, indicating a major building enterprise in a short period. Besides the large Queen Anne Style farmhouse the group includes a huge gambrel-roofed dairy barn, a circular silo of red tile, one of the few surviving hop barns and several out-buildings unified in color, form and placement.

11 CHRISTIAN CHURCH 1899
Territorial Road at Applegate Trail, Franklin

This church and the nearby Methodist Church of 1897 form an ensemble of vernacular rural church architecture which features careful construction, modest detailing and combinations of horizontal and vertical siding. The tower of the Christian church has been altered.

12 HOUSE WITH WINDMILL c.1910
29085 18th Avenue

Few windmills remain from the period prior to World War I when they were common among farm buildings. This survivor is unique for the effort given to match the style and finish of the house and for its elevated platform which recalls Dutch windmill forms.

13 **OBADIAH BEAN HOUSE AND BARNS**
c.1860, 1910
92688 River Road
Rev. Charles Hamilton Wallace, masonry
The typical vernacular gothic farmhouse features
two chimneys with Masonic motifs that are perhaps
the finest 19th century chimneys in Oregon. Two
barns illustrate form changes over time. The one
with the gabled roof was typical of the 1860s, while
the high, bell-cast shape of the other was common
to the 1910s.

BARNS

As with houses, the characteristics of barns evolve over time. Because change is so gradual and their designs simple and conservative, barns cannot be accurately dated from their appearance alone, however their ages may be approximated from their shapes.

The designs for the earliest valley barns were derived from familiar building types in the settlers' native states—types with even earlier origins in Europe and England. The barns of the 1840s-70s were organized around the movement of ox or horse teams through the barn and were characterized by low-pitched roofs on hewn frames enclosing a single story space. Original lean-tos braced the structure and buffered the weather. Even then, construction was usually contracted to experts who took six months or more to prefabricate the frame. The barn was then "raised" in a day or two by a large crew. Another six months or so of finish work was required by the builder to complete the building.

Roofs became steeper after 1870 and milled lumber began to replace hewn-frames. Some barns took advantage of hillside slopes to allow entrances at different levels. New farming techniques and machinery—particularly the hayfork lift—produced various kinds of high-profile barns after 1880.

By 1900, a more familiar form had evolved. The "Western barn" featured two-story construction permitting livestock on the ground floor to be fed from the haymow above. Now, with high eaves and ridge, the lean-tos were incorporated under a continuous roof pitch. Especially familiar now is the "hood," or canti-levered ridge, that shelters the hayfork carrier track and haydoor allowing loading operations to take place outside the barn in the mild Northwest climate. In fact, other ingenious but more subtle adaptations had been made to imported barn designs almost from the beginning in recognition of the local climate and materials.

An eastern innovation known as "plank framing" permitted more open interior space and gave rise to new forms including round barns and gambrel and bell-cast roof shapes. While these changes were fostered by improvements in volume, efficiency and economy, the appearance of their barns have often been a matter of pride with farmers. Because barns are an expression of the farmer's prosperity and of being "up to date," esthetics and considerations for style also contribute to the evolution of their form.

Some hop barns still remain in Lane County—remnants of a time when hops were a major crop. More accurately called hop driers or kilns than barns, these specialized wooden structures, with steep-pitched roofs and dramatic, tall ventilating towers, have changed little from 17th century English brick oast houses.

EAST LANE

The McKenzie Highway is much better known for its natural scenery than for the few buildings to be found along its route, although some are of special interest. The road follows the McKenzie Valley to McKenzie Pass Highway, a route that follows an earlier trail cut through 3,000-year-old lava beds. The trail was used as early as 1862 to move cattle to eastern Oregon and supplies to mining regions in Idaho. For nearly 100 years this difficult route was the area's only road over the Cascades. Because of heavy snow, it is now open only between July and October east of White Branch Camp.

Roads began moving up the lower McKenzie from the valley after 1866, opening the area to recreation and settlement. A gold strike north of Blue River contributed to early growth, later stimu-

lated by logging. Spas built around hot springs began to draw vacationers in the early 1900s.

The gold mines are worked little now and, although logging still dominates the area, the sawmills are gone. But some of the structures built in forest camps during the Great Depression and covered bridges built as late as 1966 remain to mark the special character of this part of the county.

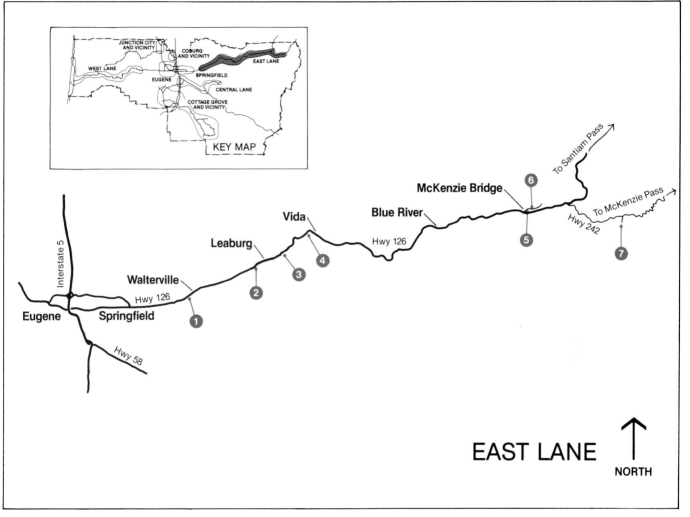

KEY MAP

JUNCTION CITY
AND VICINITY

COBURG
AND VICINITY

WEST LANE

EUGENE

SPRINGFIELD

EAST LANE

CENTRAL LANE

COTTAGE GROVE
AND VICINITY

To Santiam Pass

McKenzie Bridge

To McKenzie Pass

Blue River

Hwy 242

Vida

Hwy 126

Leaburg

Interstate 5

Walterville

Hwy 126

Eugene

Springfield

Hwy 58

EAST LANE

NORTH

2 E.W.E.B. POWER STATION 1929, 1947
POWER CANAL 1911
Highway 126, 1 mi. west of Leaburg
Lawrence & Holford, architects
Harry Poole Camden, sculptor

In this structure, with its monumental form and bas-relief depicting heroic figures, Ellis F. Lawrence found abundant architectural expression for the theme of power in the Art-Deco Style. Stylized reference to classical detail can also be seen in the fluted quarter-round column forms at the door recess and in an entablature reduced to a continuous, broad chevron band. Ordinary materials—concrete, industrial steel sash and paint—were combined in a way that lends unusual distinction to this utilitarian structure.

1 WILLIAM SMEAD FARMHOUSE 1902
39040 McKenzie Highway
.5 mi. west of Walterville

Smead replaced an earlier house on one of the valley's earliest hop farms with this house in Gothic Revival vernacular form. The beautifully intact exterior includes two bay windows with bell-cast roofs and a front porch with posts, brackets and pierced lintel screen from the Queen Anne stylebook. Smead bought the nearly completed Baker Hotel in Eugene which now bears his name, though it is popularly spelled "Smeede."

3 DUANE BISHOFF HOUSE 1903
90205 Greenwood Drive
2.6 mi. east of Leaburg

This two-story, plain-style, hip roof house is typical of its time. Larger than many, it is reputed to have served as a stage stop.

COVERED BRIDGES

Covered bridges had been a tradition in New England and Europe long before settlers arrived in Oregon to find a land thoroughly laced with rivers and streams. Dissatisfaction with the early ferries and their onerous tolls led to the first wooden bridges. In spite of tradition, the first bridges were rarely covered and their unprotected frames soon deteriorated in the wet climate of the Northwest. So it was for purely practical reasons—and not out of any sense of the picturesque—that the builders of the mid-nineteenth century began to enclose the structure of their bridges, extending their life from less than 10 years to nearly 40, barring destructive floods.

But picturesque they are and the Goodpasture Bridge shown here is one of the best known and most photographed. Built in 1938 from a design by the Oregon State Highway Department, it is one of 20 still standing in Lane County that continues a tradition into recent years. Most are later-generation bridges built from modern structural designs that, in many cases, replaced earlier bridges whose designs relied more on intuition, native genius and good luck, but which were eventually lost to age or flood. The surviving bridges range in age from the Mosby Bridge, built near Cottage Grove in 1920, to the Belknap Bridge near Blue River, built in 1966.

Perhaps no structures preserve the image of the past as much as these wonderful "airborne barns," and when they are replaced by more practical concrete spans, that image will disappear with them. It is a matter that goes beyond nostalgia since these bridges gave form to the social, economic and religious life of the early communities and, in fact, were vital to their very existence.

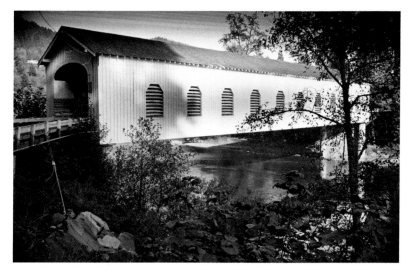

4 **GOODPASTURE COVERED BRIDGE**
1937-39
Highway 58 at Goodpasture Road,
.2 mi. west of Vida
Oregon State Highway Department, designers
Lane County, builder

5 **LOG CABIN INN** **1907**
Highway 126, McKenzie Bridge

A two-story-high porch lends a classic dignity to this Rustic Style inn—a close replica of an original (1885) stage station and resort hotel developed by George Frissel which burned in 1906. Only native materials were used in its hand-crafted construction. Walls were built of logs with saddle-notched corners and chinked with moss while poles were used for short joists and two-story-high posts. Small poles were used decoratively as railings and as siding on the gable ends where they were split and set vertically. Some of the cottages behind the main building were also built in the Rustic Style.

6 **ST. BENEDICT LODGE** **1955**
56630 North Bank Road, McKenzie Bridge
Verge & Clatworthy, architects
Gale M. Roberts Co., builder

Designed as a church, seminary and retreat, this group of simple A-frame buildings, interconnected by bridges and dramatic wooden spiral stairs, conveys a sense of informality about its use and sensitivity towards its surroundings.

7 COMMUNITY BUILDING 1930s
White Branch Organization Camp

Highway 242, 11 mi. east of McKenzie Bridge
U.S. Forest Service, designers
Civilian Conservation Corps, builders
Organizational camps were constructed only in the
Depression era and featured a community building
or lodge centrally located in a campground of
sleeping shelters and other buildings, all in Rustic
Style. (This site is leased under a special-use permit
and should be treated as private property.)

CENTRAL LANE

The Central Lane area encompasses several small communities that were founded on individual land claims and that, in each case, were given permanence by the early establishment of a post office or a school.

After coming north from California with Eugene Skinner, Elijah Bristow settled on a site that reminded him of his earlier home in Pleasant Hill, Virginia. He gave it the same name and the hewn log cabin he built there in 1846 became the first permanent homesite in Lane County.

Lowell began in 1880 as a post office on the Oregon Central Military Road near its junction with the Springfield Road. Creswell began in 1854 as the site of a post office—established not for Creswell but for Cottage Grove. That post office was eventually moved south to join the town it served and Creswell, fittingly named after the U.S. postmaster general, was founded on the same site in 1872.

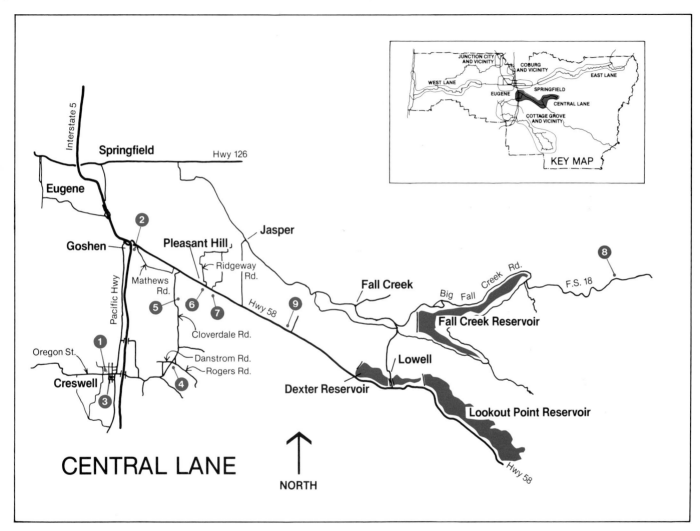

Springfield

Hwy 126

Interstate 5

Eugene

Goshen

Pacific Hwy

❷

Mathews Rd.

Pleasant Hill

Jasper

Ridgeway Rd.

❺ ❻ ❼

Hwy 58

❾

Fall Creek

Big Fall Creek Rd.

❽

F.S. 18

Fall Creek Reservoir

Oregon St.

❶

Cloverdale Rd.

Danstrom Rd.

Rogers Rd.

Creswell

❸ ❹

Lowell

Dexter Reservoir

Lookout Point Reservoir

Hwy 58

CENTRAL LANE

↑

NORTH

KEY MAP

JUNCTION CITY AND VICINITY

COBURG AND VICINITY

EAST LANE

WEST LANE

SPRINGFIELD

EUGENE

CENTRAL LANE

COTTAGE GROVE AND VICINITY

1 **METHODIST EPISCOPAL CHURCH** 1889
Now CRESWELL HISTORICAL MUSEUM
5th and West Oregon Streets, Creswell
Robert McDaniels, builder
This white picturesque gabled structure has a
number of Gothic Revival features: lancet windows,
gable panels pierced in trefoil patterns and a square
entrance tower once topped by a conical spire.
McDaniels also built the nearby Creswell Presbyterian Church (1907-08).

3 **CRESWELL SCHOOL** 1875
Now CRESWELL CIVIC IMPROVEMENT
CLUB AND LIBRARY
2nd and D Streets, Creswell
This structure typifies an institutional building form
in the last quarter of the 19th century: plain, rectangular, with its entrance front on the gable end. Early
photographs indicate the school originally was two
full stories.

2 **ANDREW J. KEENEY HOUSE** c.1875
Highway 58 at Mathews Road
.5 mi. east of Goshen
Walling's lithograph of 1884 shows that this
Missouri-born farmer's house has survived relatively
intact, although some of its detail has been
obscured by modern composition siding. The roof
shape and brick detail of this two-story house with a
long kitchen service wing indicate the vernacular
Gothic Style.

6 WM. W. BRISTOW HOUSE 1863
Highway 58 at Ridgeway Road
Pleasant Hill

One of Lane County's best examples of the Gothic Revival Style combines Gothic, Classical Revival and vernacular traditions. While the Gothic Revival Style is emphasized in the building's cruciform plan and in the scroll pattern cut into the barge boards on the gables, the front door with sidelights and square, columnar porch posts reflect Classic Revival detail.

4 CLOVERDALE METHODIST CHURCH
c. 1900
Danstrom & Rodgers Roads

This intact Gothic Revival church is almost all that remains to mark the site at Cloverdale. Its entrance facade is marked by a porch featuring an ogee arch as its lintel, a simplified rose window and a splendid belfry. A pyramidal roof of imbricated shingles covers the belfry, three flame-like crockets of wood stand on each hip and the whole is topped by a wooden crown.

5 TAYLOR BARN c.1870
84285 Cloverdale Road
2 mi. S.W. of Pleasant Hill

The Taylor barn is a mortised and tenoned hewn-frame structure. Its relatively high gable roof form and steep pitch suggest the approximate date of its construction. Such all-purpose barns were often effectively located at the edge of fields and against the uphill pastureland.

7 CHURCH OF CHRIST c.1913
Highway 58, .6 mi. east of Ridgeway Road, Pleasant Hill

This church is an interpretation of late medieval English country church architecture. Its roofs, square tower and louvered belfry form an assymetrical composition. The Tudor Style arches and heavy wood subdivisions of the window groups recall the medieval shapes interpreted here in frame construction.

8 COMMUNITY BUILDING 1936-37
Clark Creek Organizational Camp
National Forest Rt. 18, 15 mi. east of Lowell
U.S. Forest Service, designers
Civilian Conservation Corps, builders

This structure is a simple and direct statement in native materials totally appropriate to its location and use. Note the tables and benches that were rebuilt in their original form. (This site is leased under a special-use permit and should be treated as private property).

SAWMILLS

Since the 1880s when the railroad opened vast markets to the timber industry, logging has been a major factor in the growth of the county, and sawmills a common sight in both urban and rural areas. Their appearance has changed considerably over the years, however.

The movement of logs and finished lumber has always governed the location and design of sawmills. The earliest mills were often built close to timber stands and along streams that powered the saws. Away from streams, logs were moved by oxen or elaborate flumes until railroad spur lines were extended from the valley. Later mills were built closer to the railroad and sources of labor, although towns occasionally grew around the mills. Streams became less important as steam engines, fueled by wood waste, began to provide the needed power. And ponds, often man-made, were used to store logs and move them to the saws.

Roads and trucks further extended the area served by the mills, and the industry grew until 1951 when 179 sawmills were operating in Lane County, representing over 60 percent of its economy. Many of these were small concerns, often family owned, and usually without the financial resources to meet growing economic pressures.

Sources of old-growth timber were

declining, catching many mills without second-growth lands to cut. Changing economic conditions prompted some companies to consolidate into larger, automated mills closer to populated areas. Only 69 sawmills remained in 1960 when safety and environmental regulations began to force still more costly changes in logging practices and mill equipment. Without reserves to meet these demands or to sustain themselves through lean markets, the smaller mills virtually disappeared. Their loss has been more than compensated for by the 38 mills that remained in 1980—by then larger and more productive.

The physical appearance of the sawmills has also changed over time. Most millponds have been replaced by "cold decks"—stacks of logs moved around the site by mechanical stackers. Environmental concerns ended the use of wigwam burners of wood waste. The expressionless sheds that house the mill equipment were never intended as more than simple shelters—growing and changing continually as millwrights alter and add to the machinery. No mills were exempt from the pressures of change in economics and technology. They had to move or rebuild—or die. For that reason, no examples of intact early mills can be seen today.

Still relatively small and rurally located, the Bohemia, Inc. sawmill shown here is one which retains some of the components and outward appearance of earlier sawmills.

COTTAGE GROVE & VICINITY

Because it was found in solid rock rather than as gold dust in rivers, mining did not become productive until 1890 when roads and special equipment reached the mining sites of Champion, Musick, Last Chance and others. By then the mere promise of gold had already brought growth and prosperity to Cottage Grove.

As it grew at its junction of early valley roads, Cottage Grove's unique location made it a focal point for communications, mail and freight, and a center of trade for lumber, mining and farm products. As it did elsewhere, the arrival of the railroad in 1872 expanded lumber markets and many mills were built to exploit the vast local resources.

The railroad brought profound change to the form of the city as well. Its arrival caused a major shift in the center of business from its original location west of the river along River Road to the east side of the river. Here, a new "Main Street" was laid out, extending east from the river to the railroad.

The distribution of Cottage Grove's older buildings reflects this dual site history. By 1900, the area west of the river had become predominantly residential. A number of fine, late 19th century houses, many in the Queen Anne Style, can still be seen here. To the east, several of the brick buildings survive from the "later" commercial development along Main Street. Some of these, built between 1880 and about 1905, represent both the earliest and latest masonry work of Rev. Charles Hamilton Wallace.

The site chosen for Cottage Grove was ideal. To the north lay the fertile farmland of the Willamette Valley that gave promise to the town's beginnings while the Coast Range and Calapooya Mountains that extended to the west, south and east contained the gold and rich timber resources that assured its future.

The locality was settled in 1849 by survivors of a ship wrecked on a bar off the Rogue River, and who were making their way overland to Portland. They were joined by others arriving in wagon trains after 1851.

Many left for the gold fields in California after filing their land claims. Even after they returned, interest in prospecting continued, and in 1858 gold was discovered in the Calapooya Mountains.

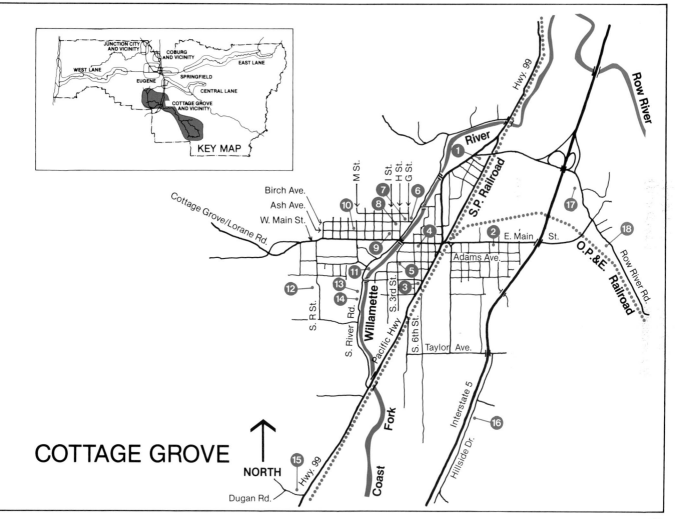

KEY MAP

JUNCTION CITY AND VICINITY
COBURG AND VICINITY
WEST LANE
EAST LANE
EUGENE
SPRINGFIELD
CENTRAL LANE
COTTAGE GROVE AND VICINITY

COTTAGE GROVE

NORTH

Cottage Grove/Lorane Rd.

Birch Ave.
Ash Ave.
W. Main St.

M St.
I St.
H St.
G St.

River

S. P. Railroad

Hwy. 99

Row River

E. Main St.

Adams Ave.

O.P.&E. Railroad

Row River Rd.

Willamette

S. R St.
S. River Rd.
S. 3rd St.
S. 6th St.

Pacific Hwy

Taylor Ave.

Coast Fork

Interstate 5

Hillside Dr.

Hwy. 99

Dugan Rd.

133

3 GEORGE AND LUCY LEA HOUSE 1891
433 S. Pacific Highway
George Lea and sons, builders

Carpenter George Lea constructed his own Queen Anne Style home. To him is attributed the craftsmanship of much of the interior and exterior woodwork, on this and several other buildings of similar quality in the Cottage Grove area, including the church at Walker.

1 BARN WITH OLD SIGN
Barn c. 1900, Sign c. 1912
N. Pacific Highway and access road to I-5
John Cochran, probable builder

''For Your Liver Dr. Pierce's Pleasant Pellets'' has given distinction and the name the ''Advertising Barn'' to an otherwise simple, commonplace board and batten structure with a hayfork gable end. It originally served the John Cochran farm.

2 JOSEPH LANDESS HOUSE c. 1925
now the ROUND-TO-IT SHOP
1551 E. Main Street
Joseph Landess, builder

A conical roof caps the original two-story cylinder of vertical wood construction strapped in place with two steel bands. The cupola and enlarged first floor are later changes. Landess was superintendent of the Champion mines.

5 **UNITED PRESBYTERIAN CHURCH** 1951
216 S. 3rd Street (NRHP)
Pietro Belluschi, architect

This church, one of Belluschi's finest buildings to
that time, is located on a corner site in a quiet older
residential neighborhood. Of note is the fenced
entry courtyard which buffers against street activity.
The clear glass windows of the sanctuary look into
this outdoor room with its bell tower. A number of
interesting houses dating from c. 1890-1910 that
surround the site are also worth seeing.

4 **FIRST NATIONAL BANK BLDG.** 1911
Corner of Sixth and Main Streets

The interior and exterior of this Neo-Classical Style
building stand essentially unaltered. It was
constructed of cream-colored brick with limestone
dressings and cornices. The building is now
occupied by independent shops and offices.

7 MARVIN DRURY HOUSE   c. 1900
704 Birch Avenue
The exterior of this small house appears historically intact. The vernacular form shows Queen Anne Style detailing in the shingle patterning on the gable ends.

6 DAVID McFARLAND HOUSE   c. 1869-70
628 Birch Avenue
The form of this home of a well-known pioneer is typical of the 1870s. Building shape and corner boards are original, but the small-paned windows and the porch are twentieth century additions.

8 OUR LADY OF PERPETUAL HELP
CATHOLIC CHURCH   1897
now the COTTAGE GROVE MUSEUM
H Street and Birch Avenue
Lee G. Hunsacker, supervisor
Michael Kebelbeck, carpenter
This church is one of a few surviving early octagonal buildings in Oregon. The stained-glass windows are reputed Italian imports. The rear tower was once taller and the present porch is not original.

10 **EUNICE AKIN HOUSE**   1904
1308 M Street
Features of the Queen Anne Style—picturesque roof
lines and shingled gable panels—were achieved
with emphatic success in Cottage Grove, especially
in small houses such as this.

9 **J.I. JONES HOUSE**   1893
39 North I Street
Crampton Jones, builder
Two tower-like turrets contribute to the complex
forms of this one-story house, long the home of the
Frank McFarland family. Queen Anne Style characteristics include the special shingling and the use of
colored glass.

12 **BOHEMIA ELEMENTARY SCHOOL** 1976
721 South R Street
Wm. W. Wilson & Assoc., architects
Vik Const. Co., builder
Designed to function either as open-plan teaching space or as a room-based school, this building was planned at a child's scale with children's needs in mind.

11 **DR. GEORGE U. SNAPP HOUSE** 1886
South River Road
This one-story Queen Anne Style House features an unusual, tall, cone-like porch roof with an adjoining gable. This gives a striking front to an otherwise modest building. The doctor used one room of the house for his office. The building has been moved here from its original location on the site of River View Terrace.

13 GLEN AND CARRY STONE HOUSE
1894-96
625 S. River Road
Glen H. Stone, builder

This Queen Anne Style house is interesting for its shingled tower and its interior woodwork, for which five kinds of lumber were imported. Stone, owner of a grist mill, helped develop the city's water company.

14 HON. ROBERT M. VEATCH HOUSE
1892-98
653 S. River Road
Rev. C.H. Wallace, mason

This Queen Anne Style house is one of a group built for prominent citizens and is notable for its simple surfaces, attic rose window and porch railing of jigsaw-work. Veatch was a veteran state legislator. The houses that now stand along River Road replaced an earlier commercial district.

15 JAMES CHAPIN HOUSE   c. 1865
77744 Dugan Road

This is a rare, early, historically unaltered, two-story house. As a late Post-Colonial Style home it exhibits characteristic crisp, plain detailing, a simple gable roof, double-hung windows with six panes in each half, and boxed-in eaves.

16 **ALEXANDER COOLEY HOUSE** 1865
2100 Hillside Drive
Zachary Shields, builder

This is one of two houses built by 14-year-old "Zach" Shields for the Cooley family. This one differs in only minor detail from another built in the same year for John Cooley, one-half mile south at 32481 Howard Loop. Both houses have two front doors—an east coast tradition. Each also features a broad roof, a gallery-like porch with square columns and exceptionally fine detail on the porch and eaves.

17 **VILLAGE GREEN MOTOR HOTEL** 1960
Row River Road near I-5
Percy Bentley, architect
W.H. Shield Const. Co., builder

With careful landscaping and deliberate building groupings, this sprawling complex attempts to create a strong sense of related spaces on a flat, undistinguished site next to the freeway. Detail of Colonial Revival origin was added to the contemporary post and lintel construction to suggest a traditional, residential character.

18 **LANE ENERGY CENTER** 1981
2915 Row River Road
Equinox Designs—G.Z. Brown & John Reynolds, architects
Archie Wynn, builder

Behind the playful false-front, inspired by old-west commercial fronts as a gesture to the commercial strip, is a much more serious array of features designed to achieve energy independence for heating and cooling. The direct gain passive design employs water barrels and a concrete floor to store heat in winter and an underground tube and roof vents to promote cooling in summer. Only a small wood stove is needed to supplement the heat provided by natural means.

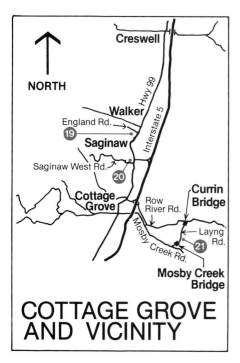

COTTAGE GROVE
AND VICINITY

19 WALKER UNION CHURCH 1895
England Road, Walker
.2 mi. west of Hwy. 99
Masonry attributed to Rev. C.H. Wallace
Carpentry attributed to George Lea and Francis Smith

A shingled, polygonal spire and a tri-part Venetian window are among the special features of this church, founded by several denominations and constructed in six months with volunteer labor. The Presbyterian Church in Eugene gave the pulpit and pews.

21 DAVID MOSBY HOUSE 1868
78067 Layng Road
Alec Spare, builder
Rev. C.H. Wallace, mason

This house is significant as a late expression of an 18th century vernacular house-type in excellent historic condition. Plain exterior detailing features the original stone foundation and brick chimneys. The interiors are also noteworthy.

20 BOOTH KELLY STORE c. 1900
Highway 99 at Saginaw
J.I. Jones, const. supervisor

This store supplied Booth Kelly loggers. Its plain, utilitarian style is characteristic of once-common country stores.

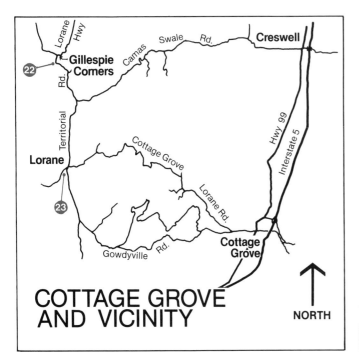

COTTAGE GROVE
AND VICINITY

NORTH

22 **DAVID ZUMWALT HOUSE (c. 1855) &
BARN (c. 1892)**
Territorial Rd., .4 mi. south of Gillespie Corners
Remarkable for its intact condition, the Zumwalt
house is handsomely sited on a small knoll just west
of the old westside Territorial Road. It is one of
Oregon's finest examples of a ''double'' or two-
front-doored house. The doors lead into two matching parlors with fireplaces on each side of a large
central chimney. The hewn frame, bricks, cedar
boards and paneled doors are all handmade
elements. The kitchen wing was added later.

23 LORANE GRANGE #54, I.O.O.F. #122, GENERAL STORE & CHRISTIAN CHURCH, c. 1900
Lorane, Oregon
Grange built by W.F. Hart

Lorane is attractive for its hillside site and neatly organized grid of streets flanking the old westside Territorial Road. Residential buildings stand close to a representative group of institutional buildings. The Christian Church, 1889, perhaps the oldest, is a simple building with fine proportions and detail including wide frieze boards and a square, louvered belfry. Three of the remaining buildings indicate in white painted shiplap siding, gables to the street, low hipped entrance porches and other ubiquitous detail the easy date of "around nineteen hundred." The more recent Post Office building adds a bit of color to the ensemble in what must be the smallest A-frame institutional structure in the world.

FOREST SERVICE STRUCTURES 1933-1942

With 44 percent of its land area divided between portions of three national forests, Lane County gained a unique architectural and historical resource in the many projects undertaken here by the Civilian Conservation Corps (CCC) for the U.S. Forest Service during the Depression era.

In addition to extensive work on timber and range lands in soil conservation and forest improvement, the CCC built thousands of structures for administrative and public use on sites throughout the country and especially in the Pacific Northwest. Almost all were built in the Rustic Style—a uniquely American design that was appropriate to Forest Service goals for a "non-intrusive" architecture closely integrated with the landscape. The style, which grew out of late-19th-century romanticism about nature and the frontier, was deliberate in its use of native materials and expressions which often emulated building techniques of the pioneers. Because it was so labor-intensive, the Rustic Style occurred on national forest lands only during the Depression.

While the program was national in scope, most decisions were made locally —a traditional process in Forest Service management. Building needs and sites were identified by personnel from each national forest. Specific designs were then prepared by architects in their regional offices, guided by general construction standards established in Washington, D.C., and by regional handbooks which described design prototypes for everything from large buildings to camp furniture. In spite of all of these standards, distinctive expressions still emerged as Forest Service architects recognized the variety of sites involved— from deep forest to rocky outcrop, and from wilderness cabin to urban headquarters—and adapted each design to the specific needs of its immediate surroundings. Further changes were often made in the field by inventive CCC crews, and today it is rare to find identical designs on different sites.

Several structures representing various building types constructed during this era and later can be seen on a tour through the Cottage Grove Ranger District of the Umpqua National Forest—a tour that includes the Bohemia mining area. *(Visitors are advised, however, that, beyond Martin Creek Road, the road to Musick and Fairview is steep, narrow and rough, and inaccessible in the winter.)* Others are listed in the sections for Central Lane and East Lane. These structures are irreplaceable and their existence provides a rare reminder of a unique period in the nation's history.

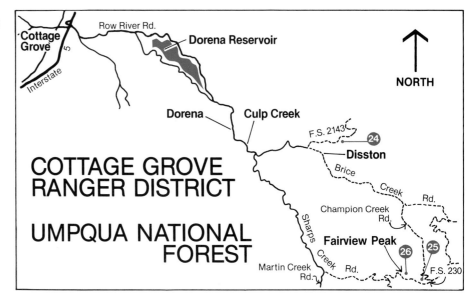

25 **MUSICK GUARD STATION** 1934
Forest Service Road 230
19.3 mi. S.E. of Culp Creek
U.S. Forest Service, designers
Civilian Conservation Corps, builders
This variant of the more typical log cabin used half-round mill ends (slab wood or cants) and peeled poles on the exterior as a more economical approach to the same visual effect.

24 **RUJADA CAMPGROUND REGISTER**
c. 1934
Forest Service Road 2143
6 mi. east of Culp Creek
U.S. Forest Service, designers
Civilian Conservation Corps, builders
Almost classical in its simple form, this handsomely proportioned log shelter had no other purpose than to record the names of visitors to this site. Regrettably, the design traditions established by structures such as this are no longer evident in the undistinguished buildings which characterize present-day forest camp architecture.

26 **FAIRVIEW LOOKOUT STATION** 1971
Forest Service Road #230
18.5 miles S.E. of Culp Creek
U.S. Forest Service, designers
Cottage Grove Const. Co., builder
Lookout stations were once common in national forests. This manned lookout station is a now-rare exception to the USFS policy of aerial surveillance. Because of its remote location and limited access, all parts were prefabricated elsewhere and assembled on site in six weeks.

While towns like Veneta and Noti were established by the eventual extension of valley settlement, communities on the western side of the Coast Range felt very little of this influence and developed independently.

Settlers arrived slowly to the isolated Florence area. The first came from the south up the coast and developed farms along the Siuslaw River and its tributaries. This same land was populated with about 50 Siuslaw Indian villages until it was appropriated by the government for white settlement in 1876. For both the Indians and the settlers the Siuslaw River was a highway of supply and communication from the coast to Mapleton.

Later settlers came from Eugene on trails cut across the mountains. Many more were attracted to Florence and other areas beyond the Willamette Valley by the Homestead Act of 1912.

Industry also grew independently along the coast. Ships connected Florence with California from 1877 on, providing instant markets for its new salmon canneries and lumber mills.

Florence's early commerce centered on the Bay Street area close to the river and waterfront. With the construction of the coast highway in the 1930s, coast communities became less isolated and new businesses located along this new source of trade.

In recent years, Florence, like so many other communities, has resurrected its original city center from the shells of a few still-standing old buildings. The riverfront along Bay Street—now known as ''Old Town''—has been given a nostalgic facelift with the relocation to the site of old buildings like the Mapleton railroad station, the construction of several ''new-old'' buildings, and particularly the restoration of the keystone in the Old Town area—the Kyle Building.

WEST LANE

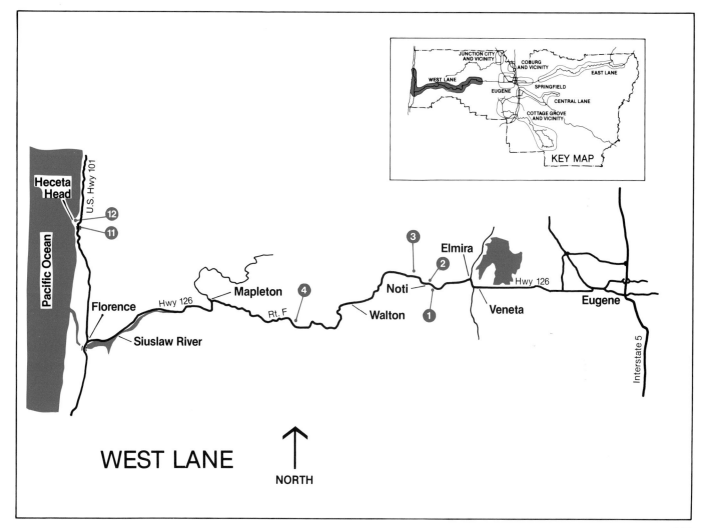

Pacific Ocean

U.S. Hwy 101

Heceta Head

⑫

⑪

Florence

Hwy 126

Mapleton

④

Rt. F

Siuslaw River

Walton

③

②

Noti

①

Elmira

Hwy 126

Veneta

Eugene

Interstate 5

WEST LANE

NORTH

KEY MAP

JUNCTION CITY
AND VICINITY

COBURG
AND VICINITY

EAST LANE

WEST LANE

EUGENE

SPRINGFIELD

CENTRAL LANE

COTTAGE GROVE
AND VICINITY

1 WILLIAM SAILOR, SENIOR, BARN 1906
22968 Highway 126, one mi. east of Noti

This 1900 stock barn is typical except for its hewn frame, rare for a building after 1890. Here, in 1912-14 were stabled six-horse teams, employed to construct the railroad from Eugene to Coos Bay.

3 FARMER HALE HOUSE 1909
Highway 126, 3.2 mi. west of Noti

This large, two-story, hipped-roof farmhouse served the stage road which once passed to its north. (Highway 126 now passes to the south.) Agricultural out-buildings indicate the use of the site since 1853 by the Hale family.

2 NOTI GRADE SCHOOL 1927
Noti

This structure with its rectangular form, hipped roof and symmetrical facade is typical of schools of the time. A three-storied, louvered central tower shelters the Colonial Style fan-lighted entrance.

4 CAMP LANE SHELTERS 1968, 1970
Highway 126, 8.5 mi. east of Mapleton
Unthank Seder Poticha Architects
Lane County & Howard Nelson Const. Co., builders

This playful collection of sleeping shelters was pre-fabricated in Eugene and lifted into place on a framework of posts on-site to avoid construction damage to the natural landscape. The result is highly sculptural and each shelter conveys the sense of a private place.

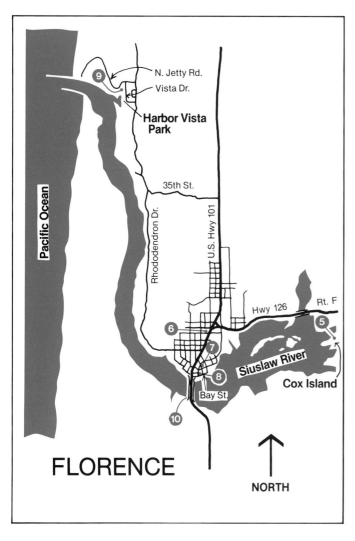

5 BENNEDICT HOUSE 1906
**Cox Island, 1.7 mi. east of Florence
(NRHP)**

The simple, rectangular forms of this two-story
house which includes a roof that extends to the
single story in the back and a central two-story enclosed ''porch'' in the front are reminiscent of an
early New England Saltbox Style. An open, Victorian
porch once surrounded the enclosed porch. Built for
Elbert Bennedict, manager of the Siuslaw Boom Co.,
the house is reputed to be the inspiration for the
Stamper house in Ken Kesey's novel *Sometimes a
Great Notion.*

6 **SIUSLAW VALLEY BANK** 1967
Highway 101 at 8th Street, Florence
Lutes & Amundsen, architects
Hiestand Const. Co., builder
Softened by careful detailing and selection of materials, the large building mass is an effective response to the broad highway space in front of the building.

7 **KENNEDY-JOHNSON HOUSE** 1892
Corner of First and Maple Street, Florence
Victor Lavio, builder
Dr. O.F. Kennedy's house stands among many older houses that formed the early residential area at the edge of the Bay Street commercial district. Its balanced, symmetrical openings, low hip roof and bracketed eaves compose a fine, rather vernacular version of the Italianate Style. It is still quite intact inside and out.

8 **WM. KYLE & SONS CO.** 1901
Now the KYLE BUILDING
1297 Bay Street, Florence (NRHP)
General store, post office, soda fountain, dance hall, roller rink—the centerpiece of Florence's early years is once more the key building in the revitalized Old Town area. The false front, so common to turn-of-the-century western buildings and handsomely detailed in the Commercial Italianate Style, announces a main building and warehouse that are still virtually intact. The interior woodwork and structure also contain details common to the period.

9 **HARBOR VISTA OVERLOOK** 1979
Harbor Vista Park at North Jetty, Florence
Briscoe and Berry, architects
Gaines Construction, builders
This simple overlook shelter frames views and protects visitors from the prevalent winds and rains of the coast. Originally built in 1973, it was destroyed by arson in 1977 and rebuilt to the original design in 1979.

11 **CAPE CREEK BRIDGE** 1931
     Highway 101 at Devils Elbow State Park
Conde B. McCullough, bridge engineer
John K. Holt, builder
Handsomely proportioned in reinforced concrete,
the classical style elements of this bridge bear
some resemblance to the Roman aquaducts though
lighter in mass. The single, large parabolic arch
spans half its length of 440 feet. A tunnel constructed in 1931 by Kern and Kibb abuts the south
end of the bridge.

10 **SIUSLAW RIVER BRIDGE** 1936
     Highway 101, Florence
Conde B. McCullough, bridge engineer
Mercer-Fraser Co., builder
This bridge is representative of many built along
Highway 101 in the 1930s employing Art-Deco
design elements. Modernistic and oriental motifs
were carefully cast in the massive reinforced concrete pylons supporting the center steel drawbridge
and also appear in the intricate iron grilles of the
entry pylons. The bridge is dramatically composed in
five parts, each distinctive in character and varying
with the structural system employed and the treatment of mass and detail. McCullough also designed
bridges at Yaquina Bay, Alsea Bay, Umpqua River
and Coos Bay under a Depression era program. All
were opened in 1936.

In its early years, this isolated site included several farm buildings which sustained the keepers' families and a single-family residence, demolished in 1940, that housed the lighthouse keeper. This keeper's house stood in the open area west of the remaining residence, a duplex that housed the 1st and 2nd assistant lighthouse keepers. Their apartments were identical in all ways but one—the dining room chandelier in the first assistant's side has one more lamp than the other. The keepers left in 1963 when the lighthouse operation was automated, and the residence was leased to Lane Community College in 1970 by the Forest Service who took over the property in 1966. All structures were built from the same design as those at Umpqua lighthouse near Reedsport.

Except for the removal of the original one-story kitchen wings at the rear, the two-and-one-half story frame residence is reasonably intact. Its modest Queen Anne detailing marks each floor in horizontal bands of shiplap siding, regular shingles and staggered shingles with stained glass windows at the upper level. The restored porch contains bead-edged balusters and a lintel screen with spindles and turned balls.

The stucco finish on the brick lighthouse is embellished with detail suggesting the Elizabethan Revival Style. It also features sandstone trim at the base and framed openings and a cast-iron interior stair and lantern railing. The attendant on duty, who was required to wind the clock every four hours, stayed in the attached one-room cottage.

12 HECETA HEAD LIGHTHOUSE 1893
ASST. LIGHTHOUSE KEEPERS' HOUSE
Highway 101 at Heceta Head (NRHP)
H.M. Montgomery & Co., builders
1981 Porch Restoration: Gilland and Peting, architects; Philip Dole, consultant; Gregg Olson, builder

SUGGESTED READING

GENERAL REFERENCE

Dicken, Samuel N. and Dicken, Emily F. *The Making of Oregon: A Study in Historical Geography.* Portland: Oregon Historical Society, 1979.

_____. *Oregon Divided: A Regional Geography.* Portland: Oregon Historical Society, 1982.

Loy, William G. *Atlas of Oregon.* Eugene: University of Oregon, 1976.

McArthur, Lewis. *Oregon Geographic Names,* 5th ed. Portland: Oregon Historical Society, 1982.

GUIDES TO ARCHITECTURAL STYLES AND FEATURES

Blumenson, John J.-G. *Identifying American Architecture: A Pictorial Guide to Styles and Terms, 1600-1945.* rev. ed. Nashville: American Association for State and Local History, 1981.

Clark, Rosalind. "Oregon Architecture: A Guide to Styles." [To be published in 1983 under the title, *Oregon Styles: Architecture 1840 to 1950.*]

Poppeliers, John et al. *What Style Is It?* Washington, D.C.: The Preservation Press of the National Trust for Historic Preservation.

Rifkind, Carole. *A Field Guide to American Architecture.* New York: New American Library, 1980.

Whiffen, Marcus. *American Architecture Since 1780: A Guide to the Styles.* Cambridge: MIT Press, 1969.

OREGON ARCHITECTURAL HISTORY

Ross, Marion D. *A Century of Architecture in Oregon, 1859-1959.* Portland: Women's Architectural League, 1959.

Statewide Inventory of Historic Sites and Buildings. Salem: Oregon State Historic Preservation Office, 1976.

Vaughan, Thomas and Ferriday, Virginia, eds. *Space, Style and Structure: Building in Northwest America.* 2 vols. Portland: Oregon Historical Society, 1974.

LANE COUNTY HISTORY AND ARCHITECTURE

Eugene Millrace: A History. Eugene: Historic Review Board.

A Guide to Historic Sites and Structures, Eugene, Oregon. Eugene: Historic Review Board.

Illustrated History of Lane County, Oregon. Portland: A.G. Walling, 1884.

Kotz, Ellen, co-ordinator. *Historic Buildings of Springfield: 1980.* Springfield: City of Springfield and Springfield Historical Commission.

Lane County Historian. Eugene: Lane County Historical Society.

Moore, Lucia W., McCormack, Nina W. and McCready, Gladys W. *The Story of Eugene.* New York: Stratford House, 1949.

Whiteaker Historic Inventory. Eugene: Historic Review Board.

[A number of pamphlets and periodicals concerning Lane County history are available at chambers of commerce and at museums and historical societies throughout the county.]

OREGON ARCHITECTS

Nelson, Lee H. "Architects of Oregon: Piper and Williams." *The Call Number* (University of Oregon). 20:2 (spring 1959), 4-15.

Stubbleline, Jo, ed. *The Northwest Architecture of Pietro Belluschi.* New York: F.W. Dodge Corp., 1953.

W.R.B. Willcox: His Architectural and Educational Theory. Eugene: Department of Architecture, University of Oregon, 1980.

SPECIAL SUBJECTS

Alexander, Christopher. *The Timeless Way of Building.* New York: Oxford University Press, 1979.
[A proposal for user-based design adopted by the University of Oregon.]

Dole, Phillip. "Farmhouse and Barn in Early Lane County," *Lane County Historian,* 10:1 (August, 1965), 23-24.

Downing, A.J. *The Architecture of Country Houses.* New York: Dover Publications, 1969).
[A reprint of an 1850 handbook.]

Guide to Public Art in Eugene. Eugene: Friends of the Museum, University of Oregon Museum of Art.
[Pamphlet which lists artwork in Eugene parks and public buildings.]

Nelson, Lee H. *Oregon Covered Bridges.* Portland: Oregon Historical Society, 1976.
[Includes information about the life and work of Lord Nelson Roney.]

INDEX

BUILDINGS & SITES